SEMEIA 19

The Book of Job
and Ricoeur's Hermeneutics

Editor of this Issue:
John Dominic Crossan

© 1981
by the Society of Biblical Literature

SEMEIA 19

Copyright © 1981 by the Society of Biblical Literature

All rights reserved. No part of this work may be reproduced or transmitted in any form or by any means, electronic or mechanical, including photocopying and recording, or by means of any information storage or retrieval system, except as may be expressly permitted by the 1976 Copyright Act or in writing from the publisher. Requests for permission should be addressed in writing to the Rights and Permissions Office, Society of Biblical Literature, 825 Houston Mill Road, Atlanta, GA 30329, USA.

ISSN 0095-571X
ISBN 978-1-58983-591-7

Printed in the United States of America
on acid-free paper

CONTENTS

Contributors to this Issue iv

PART I. INTRODUCTION

The Book of Job and Ricoeur's Hermeneutics
Loretta Dornisch 3

Paul Ricoeur and Biblical Interpretation:
A Selected Bibliography (II)
Loretta Dornisch 23

PART II. ESSAYS ON PAUL RICOEUR AND JOB 38

Job or the Impotence of Religion and Philosophy
André Lacocque 33

Job 38 and God's Rhetoric
Michael V. Fox 53

Satanic Semiotics, Jobian Jurisprudence
Richard Jacobson 63

Reading Ricoeur Reading Job
David Pellauer 73

PART III. DISCUSSIONS OF THE PRECEDING ESSAYS

The Sense of the Text and a New Vision
Frederick J. Bolton 87

Three Ways in Text Interpretation
Donald R. Buckey 91

Speech and Silence in Job
Robert Paul Dunn 99

Cosmos and Covenant
Walter James Lowe 107

The *Silence* of Job as the Key to the Text
Alan M. Olson 113

Deconstruction, Plurivocity, and Silence
Allan Patriquin 121

CONTRIBUTORS TO THIS ISSUE

Frederick J. Bolton
    Department of Religion
    St. Olaf College
    Northfield, MN 55057

Donald R. Buckey
    Department of Religion and
      Philosophy
    Mount Union College
    Alliance, OH 44601

Loretta Dornisch
    Department of Religious
      Studies
    Edgewood College
    Madison, WI 53711

Robert Paul Dunn
    Department of English
    Loma Linda University
    Riverside, CA 92505

Michael V. Fox
    Department of Hebrew and
      Semitic Studies
    University of Wisconsin-
      Madison
    Madison, WI 53706

Richard Jacobson
    Department of Comparative
      Literature
    University of Wisconsin-
      Madison
    Madison, WI 53706

André Lacocque
    Chicago Theological Seminary
    5757 S. University Avenue
    Chicago, IL 60637

Walter J. Lowe
    Candler School of Theology
    Emory University
    Atlanta, GA 30322

Alan M. Olson
    Department of Religion
    Boston University
    745 Commonwealth Avenue
    Boston, MA 02215

Allen Patriquin
    Department of Religious
      Studies
    Beloit College
    Beloit, WI 53511

David Pellauer
    Apt. 401
    99 Claremont Avenue
    New York, NY 10027

PART I
Introduction

THE BOOK OF JOB
AND RICOEUR'S HERMENEUTICS

Loretta Dornisch
Edgewood College

ABSTRACT

This study provides the background and context for applying Paul Ricoeur's hermeneutics to the book of Job. The study consists of five parts: (1) a brief description of the efforts of members of the American Academy of Religion Group on The Interpretation Theory of Paul Ricoeur, with some members of the Society of Biblical Literature, to understand and apply Ricoeur's theory; (2) a summary of some of Ricoeur's references to the book of Job; (3) an outline of those aspects of Ricoeur's work which relate explicitly to exegesis of the biblical text; (4) a sketch of some other themes of Ricoeur's developing theory which have implications for biblical studies; and (5) an introduction to the other articles in this issue.

Although he is neither exegete nor theologian, Paul Ricoeur continues to have an impact on biblical research through his efforts to develop a general theory of interpretation. For him, biblical hermeneutics is one aspect of a general theory of interpretation which has its origins in an effort to understand ordinary language as the foundation of the various developed specialized languages which we recognize in scientific as well as in poetic discourse.

1. The Study Group on the Interpretation Theory of Paul Ricoeur

Ricoeur's studies on biblical hermeneutics in *Semeia* 4 (1975a) provided the substance for a symposium in which a nuclear group discussed with Ricoeur his work on religious language and parables. Present were philosophers, theologians, exegetes, and literary critics. The interdisciplinary character of Ricoeur's work, as well as the diverse professional vocabularies of the members of the symposium, posed a challenge that was formidable but nevertheless stimulating. Therefore, under the sponsorship of the American Academy of Religion, a study group was formed which also included members of the Society of Biblical Literature. Since presentations of the first three years were largely theoretical, it was decided in 1978 to apply the theory by inviting biblical researchers with somewhat divergent approaches to address a particular text, not in order to provide an extensive exegesis, but rather to demonstrate particular approaches. The plan was to share common readings from Ricoeur's theory contained in *Interpretation Theory* (1976b), then to have each participant describe an approach and indicate how that approach would work out concretely. Respondents would add critique.

Job 38 was chosen as the text for a number of reasons: (1) Job is a key book and a perennial challenge for biblical interpretation; (2) commentaries on Job illustrate the *conflict of interpretations*, a key concept in Ricoeur's theory; (3) Job 38 is considered by a majority of commentators as the key chapter to the book of Job, and an outstanding example of *religious discourse*, another important phrase in Ricoeur's theory; and (4) Ricoeur has referred explicitly to the book of Job in a number of works.

2. Ricoeur's Explicit References to the Book of Job

Although Ricoeur has not written extensively on Job, there is substantive interpretation in *The Symbolism of Evil* (1967), as well as references in a number of other books and articles.

In *The Symbolism of Evil* Ricoeur treats of the phenomenology of confession; the three primary symbols of defilement, sin, and guilt; and four myths of the beginning and of the end, as a way into the problem of speaking about evil. Since the author of Job raises questions about the problem of evil in a narrative that has become classic, it is not surprising to find many explicit and implicit references in Ricoeur's study.

Ricoeur analyzes the symbolism of sin as a positive force under three aspects: (1) the consciousness of sin as criterion of fault (81); (2) sin as "at once and primordially personal *and* communal" (83); and (3) the hypersubjectivity of the reality of sin (84). This latter is the polarity of the absolute seeing or sight of God as wisdom and the abjectness of human being as seen by God.

> The book of Job is the witness of this crisis: Job feels the absolute seeing as an inimical seeing that causes him to suffer and finally may kill him ... the destruction of the old theory of retribution raised a doubt about this seeing, which suddenly reveals itself as the seeing of the hidden God who delivers persons to unjust suffering. [1967:85-86. I have modified the translation.]

Although we could profitably discuss other references to Job in this book (e.g., 107, 255, 324), we will emphasize here the remarks within the section, "The Reaffirmation of the Tragic" (310-26). Ricoeur uses *tragic* in the context of Aristotelian classical description. The tragic hero awakens in us once again the great tragic emotions: " ... terror and compassion, beyond all judgment and all condemnation; a *merciful* vision of human being comes to limit the accusation and save from the wrath of the Judge" (313; translation modified). In this sense there is a tragic element in biblical theology, which makes the God of the Covenant an ethical God, tending toward a "moral vision of the world" which includes the three elements of tribunal, retribution, and Judge. ("Ethical" and "moral" are used in the limiting sense associated with words such as *penal*.) However, the suffering of the innocent is a contradiction of this "moral vision":

> The book of Job is the upsetting document that records this shattering of the moral vision of the world. The figure of Job bears witness to the irreducibility of the evil of scandal to the evil of fault ... Hence, it may be asked whether the Hebrew and, more generally, the Near-Eastern theme of the "suffering Just One" does not lead back from the prophetic *accusation* to tragic *pity*. [314]

Through the dramatic movement of the dialogue, Job, "faced with the torturing absence of God, dreams of his own absence" (319); there is no answer to Job's problem: there is no solution to the problem of suffering. The questioner becomes the one questioned. It is the *innocent* Job who repents. Here we have a contradiction of terms, a paradox, a symbol. But it is the symbol which gives rise to thought. Or in later Ricoeurian terms, we have the metaphorical twist, the semantic impertinence which redescribes reality.

In the biblical corpus, Ricoeur sees this tragic contradiction transcended only in the figure of the Suffering Servant of Second Isaiah, where suffering becomes an "*action* capable of redeeming the evil" (324). Nevertheless, the question may be asked of Ricoeur if the thrust of the complete narrative of Job, including the restoration of his goods and family, does not have an implicit suggestion of the redemption motif. Ricoeur suggests as much in another context to be discussed later.

The French title *De l'interprétation. Essai sur Freud* (1970) indicates the next context for Ricoeur's efforts to extend his studies in interpretation theory. This analysis extends his critique of narcissism or false consciousness, and also enables him to see the symbolic "giving up of the father" as being at the heart of the problematic of faith (550). It is a similar struggle in which Job is engaged. Job not only refuses to submit to the false consciousness of his friends, but he also refuses to delude himself, even though such a delusion would simplify his problem.

> Job receives no explanation of his suffering; he is merely shown something of the grandeur and order of the whole, without any meaning being directly given to the finite point of view of his desire.... A path is thus opened, a path of non-narcissistic reconciliation. [548-59]

In this interpretation, there is "a certain coincidence of the tragic God of Job and the lyric God of John" (536).

Such contradiction is raised in regard to Job in similar fashion in two studies in *The Conflict of Interpretations* (1974a), "'Original Sin': A Study in Meaning," and "Religion, Atheism, and Faith." It is against the false righteousness of accusing and justifying that God speaks to Job out of the whirlwind (309). True faith is violently contrasted with the law of retribution; it is essentially a "tragic faith, beyond all assurance and protection" (455).

> It would be a faith that moves through the shadows, in a new "night of the soul" ... before a God who would not protect me but would surrender me to the dangers of a life worthy of being called human. [460]

The order spoken of in Job 38 is beyond human knowing. Nor is there any intelligible connection between the physical order and the ethical order. Revelation is in the *voice* that *speaks to* Job, so that "dialogue is in itself a mode of consolation" (461). Although the consolation of the word is not resolution, it is nevertheless revelation. The power of saying gathers the discordances of the world and gives them shape (465). Word creates and brings about the beginning of the re-newed.

In commenting on the exegesis of Genesis 1.1-2.4a (1971b), Ricoeur makes several references to Job 38. For his understanding of biblical interpretation, he uses G. von Rad's *Theology of the Old Testament* and *The Problem of the Hexateuch and Other Essays* (67, 70), as well as P. Beauchamp's *Création et Séparation* (53, 74). Following von Rad, Ricoeur recognizes the wisdom tradition of the creation motif originating in Egypt. "This reasoned, reflective theology ought to be distinguished from the faith concerning election and salvation. Measured by the grandeur of the cosmos, human being discovers himself full of fear and admiration" (70). Job 38 presents a view of the world in which the place of human being is practically nil (78). This view of creation represents a meditation on the ordering operations in creation rather than on the violent struggle characteristic of other creation motifs of the Near-East. It is a movement to the radical origin of things, not unlike the movement of modern thinkers (82-83).

"Toward a Hermeneutic of the Idea of Revelation" is the title of a more recent study of Ricoeur's on the paradox at the heart of the book of Job. Those situations "where the misery and the grandeur of human being confront each other, Hebraic wisdom interprets . . . as the annihilation of humans and the incomprehensibility of God—as the silence and absence of God" (1977c:11).

> Wisdom does not teach us how to avoid suffering, or how magically to deny it, or how to dissimulate it under an illusion. It teaches us how to endure, how to suffer suffering. It places suffering into a meaningful context by producing the active quality of suffering.
>
> This is perhaps the most profound meaning of the book of Job, the best example of wisdom (12).

The conclusion of the book of Job provides a superb example of religious discourse which moves from the poetic dialogue of complaint and argumentation, to the rhetorical voice of God out of the whirlwind, to supplication and praise. "The knowledge of how to suffer is surpassed by the lyricism of praise" (14).

These examples indicate, then, that the book of Job has been an important text for Ricoeur for the last twenty years. Though the references are not lengthy, they suggest some important directions for an interpretation of the book. They are woven throughout Ricoeur's developing theory of interpretation.

3. An Outline of Explicit References to Biblical Interpretation

Ricoeur uses many bibilical references besides those in the book of Job. The materials summarizing these references will be organized somewhat chronologically to show Ricoeur's developing thematic interests. The themes may be grouped around eight focal points of Ricoeur's studies: (1) Christian praxis; (2) the confessional literature of the Hebrew scriptures; (3) the myth of the fall and the tragic myth; (4) Genesis and structuralism; (5) demythologizing, symbols, and language theory; (6) religious language and the parables; (7) apocalyptic; and (8) revelation, the naming of God, and imagination.

Christian Praxis. Brought up in the Liberal Protestant tradition of France in the 1920's, Ricoeur was reoriented, as many others had been, by the "Barthian shock," which he experienced in 1936 when he read the French translation of Barth's commentary on Romans. The faith called for by Barth, as well as that described by Kierkegaard, continues to provide a centering point for Ricoeur. This faith is supplemented, however, by Word theologies such as those developed by Ebeling and Fuchs. Nevertheless, this faith is never in isolation, but is always in the context of a total humanity, which includes the institutions which human beings create. In "From Nation to Humanity: Task of Christians," Ricoeur wrote in 1965: "Planetary consciousness, structural obstacles, and conjunctural obstacles form a unitary constellation, which first calls for an analysis and then an acceptance of responsibility" (1974c:134). *Analysis* and *responsibility*—these are the two prongs of the task. The biblical texts give nourishment, reflection, and meditation for such analysis and responsibility (1965:98). Such texts communicate a message, a call to me, a *kerygma* (1978f:213); thus the text is never a dead letter. It is always a call for personal response, but within the context of history, culture, and human institutions, including politics and the state. For Ricoeur, then, Job is never read merely as an interesting middle Eastern "romance." If the text is interpreted, it calls for a response. In fact, the interpreting is a response.

The Confessional Literature of the Hebrew Scriptures. Ricoeur's analysis of ancient mid-Eastern confessional literature led him to a meditation on the primary and privileged symbols of *defilement*, *sin*, and *guilt*.

> It can be said, in very general terms, that guilt designates the *subjective* moment in fault as sin is its *ontological* moment. Sin designates the real situation of human being before God, whatever consciousness the person may have of it. . . . To be guilty is . . . to be ready to undergo the chastisement. . . . [1967:101–102. Translation modified.]

This is the paradoxical situation in which the problem of Job arises. Through the dialogues, Job's friends argue for a causal relationship between Job's responsibility and the evil which befalls him. It is such responsibility and guilt which Job refuses to accept. In the epilogue, however, he accepts responsibility for and repents for an earlier attitude (Pope: 290) which he now rejects and despises, having "seen Yahweh with his own eyes." In Ricoeur's terminology, Job is accepting "the real situation of human being before God," the situation of sinfulness before the Totally Other, the Holy.

The Myth of the Fall and the Tragic Myth. Ricoeur studies four types of representing the beginning and the end of evil. Two especially are helpful in a dialectic with the book of Job: (1) the myth of the fall, and (2) the tragic myth. Job's "fall," like Adam's, is against the backdrop of a perfect creation, but the problem of reponsibility is handled very differently. It is clear that Eve and Adam are responsible, through their actions, for bringing about suffering and evil, although, at the same time, evil was already there, represented by the serpent. In a similar way, in the Job framework, there is an outside tempter, a satan, and a "fall" from well-being, but the complexity and the subtlety of the questions raised in the poetic dialogues are of a far different order in the book of Job from what they are in the dialogues of the Genesis stories.

Likewise, as a number of interpreters have pointed out, there are parallels between the tragic myths of Greek tragedy and the book of Job. The Greek motif includes "the god who tempts, blinds, and leads astray" (1967:173). The book of Job also describes a god who tempts, brings about terrible sufferings, and may kill his victim. But, on the one hand, Greek tragedy describes a hero who, though he has not committed the fault, is nevertheless guilty. In contrast, Job neither has committed fault, nor will he accept guilt in relationship to his suffering. His refusal makes possible another kind of deliverance.

> There is a tragic salvation, which consists in a sort of aesthetic deliverance issuing from the tragic spectacle itself, internalized in the depths of existence and converted into pity with respect to oneself. Salvation of this sort makes freedom coincide with understood necessity. [1967:173]

It is in this sense that Job has affinities with the heroes of Greek tragedy.

Genesis and Structuralism. In 1969, Ricoeur was invited by the French Catholic Association for the Study of the Bible to make several presentations at their second annual congress. Other participants included Roland Barthes and Louis Marin. Robert M. Polzin considers Ricoeur's introductory paper "a splendid introduction to methodology in biblical exegesis" (Polzin: 202).

This introductory paper is titled "Du conflit à la convergence des méthodes en exégèse biblique" (1971a). In Ricoeur's view, one advantage of biblical criticism in the development of interpretation theory is that the biblical field is defined by its formal object, the biblical literature. On the other hand, it is a field polarized by different methods. Ricoeur shows that these different methods need not remain in unresolved conflict. On the contrary, properly understood, they may be seen as converging.

Ricoeur proposes three moments for his analysis: (1) the historical-critical method as practiced by von Rad; (2) the semiological model derived from Barthes; and (3) interpretation as Ricoeur is developing his theory. After carefully unfolding the implicit structures of the first two approaches, Ricoeur points out how an author such as von Rad uses an implicit structural analysis of the accounts of the faith of Israel. A rereading of von Rad, using the distinctions of three levels elaborated by Barthes: (1) the level of functions; (2) the level of actions; and (3) the level of the narrative (44), then reveals an implicit structural analysis which von Rad had developed out of the materials.

One is then able to ask the question of the relationship of methods. It is such a question which focuses the hermeneutic problem. What is an exegete such as von Rad doing when he uses an historical-critical or genetic method? What is a structuralist such as Barthes doing in his semiotic analysis?

A key is found in *writing*, or discourse committed to a text. Four characteristics of a written text are important to note. (1) It is the intentional meaning which is inscribed. (2) At the same time, writing detaches the meaning of the discourse from dependence on the writer.

The text is then freed for other times and places (48). (3) Such writing profoundly alters the referential function. The reference is freed from the ostensive limitations of the time and place of origin because the time and place of the original discourse no longer exist. This is not to absolutize the text; nor is it to overlook the historical, literary, philological, sociological, and cultural studies which help us better to understand a text. On the contrary, such studies are crucial. Nevertheless, the writing of a poem frees its author's meaning so that the meaning can survive, that is, live beyond the author. "A text carries its own referents" (49), so that its "world"—the Greek "world," the Johannine "world," or the "world" of Job—unfolds in front of the text, much as a "world" unfolds in front of a screen on which we have projected a slide. We can see there a "world" which has been "caught" in action, and thereby rendered available to us in the future. (4) Finally, for a written text, the intended audience is anyone who is given the ability to read the text. The text is addressed to all those readers who are able to bring out its meaning.

Such reading is not subjective in a narrow sense, because it requires validation, a logic of probability, parallel to a logic of empirical verification. Each method of interpreting a text has its own presuppositions, procedures, and methods of validation. Insofar as the validations of diverse methodologies move toward concurrence, there is a *convergence* rather than a *conflict of interpretations*.

In a subsequent presentation at the same conference, Ricoeur applies his theory to an exegesis of Genesis 1.1–2.4 in the hope of showing the possibility of a *convergence* of methods (1971b). He uses first the genetic technique of von Rad complemented by that of Werner H. Schmidt (73). Then he recognizes the structuralist's desire to analyze the text as a synchronic whole, rather than in its genetic parts, in order better to see the relationship of the parts to the whole. Repeated phrases, e.g., "and God said . . ."; series of parallel objects: light, sky, earth; sequences, e.g., "On the first day"; turning points, e.g., "the fourth day"; are all structures the analyst looks for, notes, or questions in relation to the whole.

Having applied each of the two methods, Ricoeur then asks a key question for interpretation: "Who interprets? the theologian or the philosopher? the preacher or the exegete before him? . . . There does not exist an innocent interpretation" (80). It is the structure, whether analyzed genetically or semiotically, which carries the interpretation, so that, when we interpret out of a tradition, we appropriate the meaning of the text, that is, we make it our own in some way. Ricoeur interprets both from within the historical-critical tradition and from within a semiotic tradition. As he sees it, the two methods do not necessarily contradict each other, but, on the contrary, they complement and affirm each other at many points. In fact, for Ricoeur the convergence of the two methods brings together the two streams of Hebrew reflection, the historical tradition and the wisdom tradition, precisely by using a reflective enumeration of the cosmic elements of Genesis 1, rather than by using a violent separation of the cosmic elements such as we may have expected from other examples of the Near-Eastern creation genre (83).

In a third presentation at that same conference (1971c), Ricoeur insists that we are always interpreting out of a tradition.

> We belong to the same tradition as the text: interpretation and tradition are the inside and the outside of the same historicity. Interpretation is applied to a tradition and makes tradition itself. The text is the reconstruction of a tradition and the interpretation is the reconstruction of the text. [291]

For Ricoeur, the historical-critical method is irreplacable; nevertheless, it ought to be corrected by the overcoming of three illusions: the illusion of the source, the illusion of the author, and the illusion of the audience (292). The origin of the text is itself a function of the text, not a solution to the text. The diachronic dimension—its history—remains a part of the text. There is no text without an author, a person or persons who wrote the text. Nevertheless, we do not have access to the psychology, the experience, or the intention of the author or authors except through the text and the world it signifies. In the same way, we do not have access to an "original audience or addressee" except through the text which we have here and now.

> This is the signification of the text: to know the "work" of meaning in the dialectic of tradition-interpretation, of which the actual text is the result. [293]

Interpretation of a text is neither one nor multiple. There are always many possibilities of reading a text, but the ways are not infinite. Moreover, the field of possible interpretations is always limited by the communitarian character of interpretation of which an individual exegesis is a part (295).

What does this mean, then, for an interpretation of the book of Job? The following conclusions may be drawn: (1) Different methods of interpreting Job need not necessarily conflict; on the contrary, properly understood, they may well converge. (2) Job 38 is a written text in which the intentional meaning is inscribed. It projects its own "world" which we interpret. If we are able to read, it is addressed to us, though obviously it carries genetic and structural components which are important to our interpretation. (3) In spite of different approaches to interpretation, we can aim for a validation, a logic of probable interpretation, a convergence rather than a conflict of interpretations. (4) While making use of historical and sociological tools, we should at the same time avoid the illusions of the source, the author, and the audience, as end-goals of textual interpretation. (5) There are many possible interpretations of Job 38, but these are limited by the continuing history of the text itself, in the dialectic of tradition and interpretation, a dialectic and a history which we are continuing into the future.

Demythologizing, Symbol, and Language Theory. Study of the biblical scriptures was an important part of the development of Ricoeur's theory of symbol, interpretation, and language. Three articles reflect this break-through: (1) a preface to Bultmann's *Jésus, mythologie et démythologisation* (1974a:381–401); (2) a study of original sin (269–86); and (3) a study on the symbol of fatherhood (468–97).

Ricoeur thinks both with and against Bultmann. With him, he believes that a "text accomplishes its meaning only in personal appropriation. . . . The moment of exegesis is not that of existential decision but that of 'meaning'" (397). Nevertheless, this moment of meaning must be distinguished from that of signification, the "moment when the reader grasps the meaning," when the meaning is actualized for the reader. According to Ricoeur, Bultmann's theory of interpretation moves too quickly to decision, neglecting the objectivity of the moment of meaning. The semantic must precede the existential. In Ricoeur's view, Bultmannians move from exegesis to the existential or to the theological without asking what happens in between. Bultmann lacks a sufficiently developed language theory.

In pursuit of such a language theory, Ricoeur studied in two separate articles the symbol of original sin as used by Augustine and the symbol of fatherhood as used by Jesus. Augustine's temptation, as well as common usage in the churches, makes the symbol of original sin an idol and thereby deprives it of its fullness of meaning. To miss the symbol is to succumb to the legalistic temptation of "Job's friends, who explain to the suffering just man the justice of his sufferings" (281). What Ricoeur says of the symbolic function of the story of the Fall may be said of the story of Job:

> This story has an extraordinary symbolic power because it condenses in an *archetype* of human being everything which the believer experiences in a fugitive fashion and confesses in an allusive way. Far from explaining anything at all . . . this story expresses . . . the unexpressed essence of human experience—which is inexpressible in direct and clear language. [283. Translation modified.]

In one way, the movement provided by Ricoeur in his meditation on "Fatherhood: From Phantasm to Symbol," is a movement parallel with that provided by the author of the book of Job. In the beginning of each movement, there is concrete imagery followed by a question. In the working through of that question, a transformation takes place. One has moved from a language too narrow, which denies the fullness of meaning, to a fullness of language which is symbolic. As the language is transformed, so is the subject of the narrative. As Job's language changes, so does Job. In similar fashion, the reader who follows through with Ricoeur or with the author of Job finds that language transforms imagery as well as existence. The fullness of language at the end of the process is ontologically different from what it was at the beginning.

Religious Language and the Parables: A seminar on religious language taught with Norman Perrin (Perrin: 1976) and David Tracy at the University of Chicago was the occasion for three of Ricoeur's lectures which subsequently appeared in *Semeia* 4, and which reflect a further development of Ricoeur's theory of language and interpretation. The first article, on the narrative form, emphasizes a structuralist approach. The second uses the metaphorical process as a focus on poetics. The third, on the specificity of religious language, completes the analysis.

In the first of these, Ricoeur concludes that the "object of hermeneutics is not the 'text' but the text as discourse or discourse as the text" (1975a:67). "Language or discourse has a speaker, a world, and a vis-à-vis. These ... constitute discourse as an 'event.'" What Ricoeur says of discourse in general, we may also say of the book of Job: "The speaker is brought to language; a dimension of the world is brought to language; and a dialogue beween human beings is brought to language" (66). But a generative code such as a narrative gives a particular characteristic to the discourse event. In this way, the narrative development itself is the message. So, too, with the book of Job. The narrative development *is* the message in a way similar to the narrative development of parable as message. Whatever may be the genetic development of the prose framework and the poetic dialogues of Job, the narrative code embracing them both cannot be ignored. On the contrary, it is the foundation structure, a point overlooked by commentators who treat the parts separately, but do not note the narrative dynamics of the whole.

In his second article on religious discourse in the parables, Ricoeur develops his thesis that metaphor is more than an ornamental figure. Metaphor makes language new and thereby redefines reality (75). Metaphor does not provide a scale model, nor an analogical model, but a theoretical model which creates a tension of terms by applying the terms to new objects or experiences, thus splitting the reference into an "ordinary" reference and a new reference. In Ricoeur's view, the narrative structure of the parable accomplishes this "metaphorical twist" by means of a language of extravagance that describes a new vision of reality. In the narrative structure of Job, too, there is a similar metaphorical twist which carries us from an initial situation through complex processes of describing and redescribing reality, reaching a climax in Job 38, where the rhetorical shift is so dramatic as to bring about a new vision of reality.

The "extraordinary in the ordinary" (115) in the dénouement of the parables creates such an extravagance that it brings about a "reorientation by disorientation" (114). This is religious language which redescribes human experience (127), particularly the human experience of the limit-situations of suffering and death. In an amazing way the author of the book of Job achieves this reorientation by disorientation. The author begins with the framework of a fable, then continues in the "ordinary" dialogues of Job, the sufferer, with his friends. But the network of questions moves through the dialogues in such a way as to intensify the limit-situations of suffering, struggle, and death, and then to disorient by exposing the weaknesses and fallacies of the traditional cause-effect views on human suffering and the problem of the relationship of suffering to God. Job 38 is a magnificent example of religious language which climactically presents the *extraordinary in the ordinary* and thereby *reorients by disorientation*. What the voice out of the whirlwind refers to is a view of reality which reflects the extraordinary in the ordinary. The voice speaks in a language which manifests the limit, boundary, or religious dimension in ordinary experience.

Apocalyptic. A foreword to André Lacocque's commentary on the book of Daniel (1979a) provided the occasion for Ricoeur to reflect again on apocalyptic in the context of a theory of interpretation. (Earlier reflections appeared, for example, in *The Symbolism of Evil* [1967: 67–70]). In his customary way, Ricoeur indicates his respect for the work of the historical-critical exegete, but points out that the work of the exegete leads to questions and interpretations the exegete sometimes does not make explicit. Ricoeur asks if a premature identification by some exegetes, for example, of the figures in Daniel, does not risk cutting off the very symbolic interpretation which the author of Daniel seems to call for (1979a:xxii). Similarly, does not an identification of the *son-of-man* figure with Israel cut off the possibilities of broader associations signaled by Isaiah and Ezechiel? An understanding of symbolic theory would allow rather for the play of various levels of interpretation, without narrowing the meaning only to a possible historical identification. The author of Daniel uses spontaneously a "movement of analogical assimilation ... a process of symbolization" (xxiii), which the exegete distorts if he too easily yields to systematization. Perhaps most important, however, is Ricoeur's comment that the book of Daniel "exhorts ... calls for martyrdom, and ... gives courage" (xxv).

A parallel critique may be offered to standard interpretations of the book of Job. Are we not sometimes tempted to a systematization which precludes the play of symbolic meaning on multiple levels? Do we not sometimes let historicism, or the genetic problem, or awareness of internal inconsistencies in the text, interfere with our understanding of the many levels of meaning, the intended symbolic or paradoxical incongruities, and even the resistance to systematization, all of which are precisely ways the author uses to communicate the complexity and the ambiguity of the human condition?

Revelation, the Naming of God, and Imagination.

> What did Job "see"? ... The orders of creation? No. His questions about justice are undoubtedly left without an answer. But ... by repenting for his supposition that existence does not make sense, Job presupposes an unsuspected meaning which cannot be transcribed by speech or *logos* a human being may have at his disposal. ... What is revealed is the possibility of hope in spite of. ... This possibility may still be expressed in the terms of a design, but of an unassignable design, a design which is God's secret. [1977c:12-13]

The idea of revelation differs as it appears in narrative, prophetic, prescriptive, or wisdom discourse. In the latter, the sage knows that somehow wisdom has preceded and that it is through participation that a person is said to be wise. "Nothing is further from the spirit of the sages than the idea of an autonomy of thinking, a humanism of the good life. ... This is why wisdom is held to be a gift of God" (13). Job moves through a false sense of his autonomy of thinking to a broader horizon, where he recognizes that for him to comprehend the universe and the totality of human experience, which is to understand suffering, is to make his god too small. To gird his loins and to stand up like a man is, on the contrary, to see as God sees, a much larger enterprise, and one that is much more humbling. Here truth is not something which can be verified scientifically. Rather, it is a "manifestation, i.e., letting what shows itself be. What shows itself is in each instance a proposed world, a world I may inhabit and wherein I can project my ownmost possibilities" (25). Such is the revelation and manifestation in Job. A world shows itself: a new way of being presents itself as possibility.

Wisdom is that aspect of revelation and of the human condition which "is directly addressed to the sense and nonsense of existence. It is a struggle for sense in spite of nonsense" (1979c:221). In contrast with the narrative, prophetic, and prescriptive forms of discourse, wisdom is often more cautious about the naming of God. This is the struggle in which Job is engaged. His friends too easily name the God of his suffering. With all his being, Job resists this blasphemy. From his experience, he knows it not to be true. Such naming of God is idol rather than manifestation. The voice out of the whirlwind *manifests* a *hidden* God. This is the paradox. In his suffering, Job acknowledges the paradox. He feels addressed. He responds to the one who has addressed him. He is called to give testimony to this manifestation, to the truth of his experience. "Only testimony that is singular in each instance confers the sanction of reality on ideas, ideals, and ways of being that the symbol depicts to us and which we uncover as our ownmost possibilities" (1977c:32-33).

In his study, "The Bible and the Imagination," (1980a) Ricoeur draws on a semiotic analysis of two parables, those of the wicked husbandmen and of the sower in Mark, to begin a process which goes beyond his earlier study of parables in *Semeia* 4. Here he conceives of the imagination as a rule-governed form of invention linked to the redescriptive power of fiction. The study emphasizes the importance of intertextuality and metaphorization in the use of the imagination in biblical interpretation.

This outline of some explicit references to biblical interpretation in Ricoeur's work makes clear how extensively his theory has already been developed, and how closely his theory is related to biblical interpretation. Although the philosophic language may at times be formidable, Ricoeur's analyses: (1) offer a foundation for a theory of interpretation that is needed in biblical studies today; (2) provide a bridge for moving from a continuing conflict of interpretations, often polarized and detrimental to one another, to a much more productive convergence of interpretations; (3) raise theoretical and practical questions which exegetes ignore to their own loss and to the loss of those who depend on them.

4. Other Ricoeurian Themes with Implications for Biblical Studies

Although it may not be immediately apparent, all of Ricoeur's works have implications for biblical interpretation, precisely because they are part of a philosophical anthropology and of a general theory of interpretation. Obviously, it is not within the scope of this study to demonstrate those implications. Nevertheless, it is those parts of Ricoeur's work which are more philosophical in tone, and therefore less available to some exegetes, which have the most far-reaching implications for biblical studies. There have been some hints of this in the questions already raised in this article in connection with symbol, language theory, and validation. This section sketches some key aspects of Ricoeur's developing theory, organized around five themes: (1) symbol; (2) explanation-understanding; (3) metaphor; (4) narrative; and (5) imagination.

Symbol. Though analyzed more fully in certain parts of his writings, Ricoeur's theory of symbol penetrates almost all of his work, sometimes without the explicit use of the word symbol. Dialectic with the works of Jaspers, Freud, Eliade, and Pierce has continued to renew Ricoeur's appreciation of the power of symbol (see 1967, 1970, 1976b; also Dornisch).

> The interpretation of symbols is not the whole of hermeneutics, but . . . it is the condensation point and . . . the place of greatest density, because it is in the symbol that language is revealed in its strongest force and with its greatest fullness. It says something independently of me, and it says more than I can

understand. The symbol is surely the privileged place of the experience of the surplus of meaning. [1971e:xvi–vii]

A controversial element in Ricoeur's theory of symbol is that of "split-reference." Structuralists, the new critics in France, and English and American proponents of logical positivism deny any reference for a text. Ricoeur, following Roman Jakobson and Northrop Frye, makes a strong case against such denial of reference. Split reference is related to that quality of the poetic which is thick, ambiguous, that is, double or multi-sensed. Such ambiguity affects all elements of communication. Ricoeur quotes Jakobson:

> The double-sensed message finds correspondence in a split addresser, in a split addressee, and what is more in a split reference, as is cogently exposed in the preamble to fairy tales of various peoples, for instance, in the usual exordium of the Majorca storytellers: " . . . It was and it was not." [Quoted in 1977b:224]

At stake is the meaning of the words *reality* and *truth* (229).

> All language, all symbolism consists in "remaking reality" . . . It is when symbolism breaks through its acquired limits and conquers new territory that we understand the breadth of its ordinary scope. [237]

This is the kind of theory that would profitably be applied to the book of Job. To discover the reference or references of Job, to unlock the symbolic discourse is the challenge for interpretation. It is the thickness of the communication which is the challenge and part of the reason why the interpretation of Job is never completed. Because the symbol gives rise to thought, it requires interpretation. The text of Job provides a theoretical model of reality which is multi-leveled, with cosmic, oneiric, and poetic aspects which have not been exhausted in spite of all the interpretations over the centuries. As a theoretical model of reality, the book of Job challenges the reader, and thereby offers the possibility of making Job a living text. Job is poetry as creation in the ontological sense of the word.

Explanation-Understanding.

> Interpretation in its last stage wants to equalize, to render contemporaneous, to assimilate in the sense of making similar. This goal is achieved insofar as interpretation actualizes the meaning of the text for the present reader. [1976b:92]

But the goal of interpretation is governed by the relationship of explanation and understanding. This relationship poses an old problem, of course, a problem with a long history which the Romanticist tradition, the questions raised by Schleiermacher, Dilthey, and others, has focused in modern times (75). With the benefit of modern linguistic theory, Ricoeur has substantially advanced the discussion. Ricoeur draws on language theory as developed by Heidegger and Wittgenstein, and model theory as developed by Hesse and Kuhn, which have shown the limitations of *explanation* as limited within the older traditions of the natural sciences. *Explanation* rather pertains to the nature of language itself, and, for *critical interpretation,* draws on theoretical language studies, on philology, on literary criticism, on structuralism, on epistemology, on historical-critical methods, on sociological and cultural studies, on whatever human disciplines can legitimately research the meaning of the text. On the other hand, each method of explanation has its own implicit understanding, whether recognized or not, because explanation and understanding are constantly in dialectic. It is precisely this dialectic which is interpretation (74). Understanding begins as a guess, moves through a complex set of procedures, involving a dialectic of explanation-and-continually-developing-understanding, and reaches a state of conclusion at the level of appropriation. Such a process moves from guess to validation, using a logic of probability along the lines developed by E. D. Hirsch (78).

For the most part, interpreters of Job have assumed the autonomy of the explanatory and understanding modes they were using. Within the German hermeneutical traditions of historical-critical method, source criticism, tradition criticism, and redaction criticism, "explanation" tended to be "scientific," with the presumption of "scientific understanding" as a correlate. "Interpretation" typically would include a theological introduction, notes, interpolations, or commentary. Ricoeur postulates that such philological, literary, or theological "explanations" carry their own understandings and interpretations. Of every exegete Ricoeur asks: What are your presuppositions? What is the hermeneutical theory which you are explicitly or implicitly using? The answer begins a dialogue which makes possible a convergence, rather than a polarizing and a continuing divergence of interpretations. Rather than dissolving the traditional exegetical methods, or ignoring the new ones, such a dialogue frees each exegete to use his or her method more effectively in dialectic with those of others.

Ricoeur's insight is that our understanding of interpretation lies in the understanding of ordinary language usage (12). He asks: What happens when I speak to you? A message is transmitted from speaker to hearer, involving a complex of moments of explanation-understanding, that is, interpretation, throughout the process. In the special case of a written text, the references are interpreted by whatever methodologies or approaches can move toward validation of meaning.

Metaphor. It is metaphor, however, which provides for Ricoeur a key to the process of ordinary language, because the metaphor is the place of the creation of new language, new meaning, new being. In *The Rule of Metaphor* Ricoeur reflects on the creation of meaning which takes place in language. Since the study has been well analyzed elsewhere (Gerhart, Lechner), it will be sufficient here to suggest application of some of the theses to the book of Job. The moment of metaphor permeates both the prose and poetic sections of Job and is important in a consideration of the relationship of the one to the other. The book of Job does not reduce to allegorical translation because such translation destroys the meaning. In fact, each interpretation, whether it be Archibald MacLeish's version, *J. B.*, or Neil Simon's *God's Favorite*, or one of the interpretations or analyses offered in biblical commentaries, partly misses the mark because the text is irreducible, even though such interpretations are necessary and helpful for a continually renewed appreciation of Job. Many of the lines of the book of Job, many of the individual speeches, many of the sections are understood only within the process of metaphorical language. Philology, history, and other disciplines, can help us better understand the metaphor, but they cannot translate the metaphor nor substitute for it.

Narrative. In what sense is the book of Job a narrative? And how does this affect our understanding of its meaning? Ricoeur presently is working to understand what happens in the narrative. In a lecture given at Emory University in 1977, he outlined a general theory of narrative discourse which offers some theses for a new look at the narrative possibilities in the book of Job. "To follow a story . . . is to understand the successive actions, thoughts, and feelings as having a particular directedness" (1978d:182). But "explanations . . . have to be woven into the narrative texture" (183). All narratives combine chronological and non-chronological aspects. In fact, "Every narrative may be seen as a competition between its episodic and its configurational dimension, between its sequence and its pattern" (184). Ricoeur feels that a key to understanding narrative is to understand the relationship between its two modes, history and fiction. "Only history may articulate its referential claim in compliance with rules of evidence common to the whole body of science" (194) and thereby claim a truth-adequation. But fictional narratives have another kind of truth-claim, based on their redescriptions of reality "according to the symbolic structures of the fiction" (195). Ricoeur suggests that both modes may be equally true, but in different ways related to their different referential claims. Few modern commentators have made historical truth-claims for the book of Job, but we may well ask how seriously some have taken the fictional truth-claims. Is Job just an interesting tale with some beautiful poetic dialogues, or merely an exercise book in philology, or does it incorporate truth about human experience which is important to human beings today? Do the various relationships of the framework and the discourse give a particular directedness to the narrative which encodes the message of the book? What is the relationship between the sequence of action-discourse and the pattern or configuration which is created? What transformation of values takes place as the narrative unfolds (197)?

> Meaning in a work of narrative art is a function of the relationship between two worlds: the fictional world created by the author and the "real" world, the apprehendable universe. [199]

Imagination. A theory of metaphor and a theory of narrative raise the problem of imagination. What is imagination? Is it just the power of forming images of things which are absent? In what way is imagination a method of creating

> a free play of possibilities in a state of non-commitment with regard to the world of perception or action? In this state of noncommitment, we try out new values, new ways of being-in-and-belonging-to-the-world. [1978i:9]

Precisely because the imagination frees itself from the confines of "reality," it is freed for another referential force, more primordial, more related to our basic belonging in a life world. It frees us from the symbols history has created for us, and gives us power to recreate that history by creating a new reality. This is the heuristic quality characteristic of fictions and of models. Precisely what is redescribed or made new are human actions, so that imagination is projective of human actions. In imagination, "I try out my ability to do something"(12). The imagination is the link of the analogical bond by which I link my "I" to the "I" of other selves, contemporary or distant.

> To put it in the idiom of competence and performance, the imagination's competence is to preserve and to identify in all our relations with our contemporaries, our predecessors, and our successors, the *analogy of the ego*. Its competence, consequently, is to preserve and to identify the difference between the course of history and the course of things. [15]

We can be affected insofar as we use our imagination to be affected. In society, our imaginations construct the ideologies out of which we live our lives. But it is also possible to use our imaginations to construct the utopia, the "no place," which, on the one hand, it is true, can generate the escapism of schizophrenia, but which, on the other hand, can also generate the new model of reality, the new symbolic structures which make a new society and new ways of thinking.

Is such a process not what is happening in the book of Job? At the beginning, the story projects a world, an ideology, in which a "truth" is assumed about the nature of suffering and its relationship to God. Job's imagination, precisely because of his suffering, does not find the prevalent ideologies truthful. In spite of the fact that he has no other models, in spite of the fact of his continuing suffering, in spite of the remonstrations of his friends and his wife, Job's imagination stretches toward another way of seeing, another set of symbolic structures. The answers proposed are inadequate to his questions. He does not find another model which satisfies his questions, but he does push his questioning to a boundary, a limit, a new horizon, a utopia, a "no place," where at least the question is not denied, where the perspective of a continuing universe of which he is a part, shows that his question is just one of many. To see is not to see. To know is not to know. Wisdom is in knowing that which is not known.

We have highlighted here some of the motifs of Ricoeur's developing theory which have important implications for biblical interpretation: symbol, the dialectic of explanation-understanding, metaphor, narrative, and imagination. These provide theoretical foundations important to an interpretation of the book of Job.

5.   An Introduction to the Other Articles in This Issue

The plan of these articles is simple. Against the background of Ricoeur's volume, *Interpretation Theory* (1976b), each author indicates the approach he would take in an exegesis of Job 38. This is to follow Ricoeur's own frequently articulated suggestion that the test of a theory is in its application. These papers are not the test, but point a direction: from a conflict of interpretations toward a convergence of interpretations. The participants reflect diverse backgrounds: biblical scholarship, semiotics, phenomenology, theology, literature, as well as differing exegetical and religious traditions and commitments. In addition, there is a wide difference in exegetical, literary, and philosophical competencies. Because of these differences, the general expectation is that of conflict. To our surprise, the discussion moves, without loss of the importance and uniqueness of each person's contributions, from a point of expected conflict closer to a possible convergence of interpretation, the aim of much of Ricoeur's work, and the hope of many who study the biblical texts.

PAUL RICOEUR AND BIBLICAL INTERPRETATION: A SELECTED BIBLIOGRAPHY (II)

Loretta Dornisch
Edgewood College

Items include works referred to in the previous article as well as pertinent and updated bibliography not included in *Semeia* 4. English translations with English publication dates are preferred when available, and excessive duplication of content is avoided.

PRIMARY SOURCES

1965   *History and Truth.* Trans. C. Kelbley. Evanston, IL: Northwestern University Press.

1967   *The Symbolism of Evil.* Trans. E. Buchanan. Boston: Beacon Press.

1968   "Contribution d'une réflexion sur le langage à une théologie de la parole." *Revue de théologie et de philosophie* 18:333–48.

1969   "Conclusions." Pp. 190–209 in *Vérité et vérification. Wahrheit und Verifikation.* Ed. H. L. Van Breda. The Hague: Nijhoff.

1970	*Freud and Philosophy*. Trans. D. Savage. New Haven, CT: Yale University Press. (*De l'interprétation. Essai sur Freud*. Paris: Seuil, 1965.)
1971a	"Du conflit à la convergence des méthodes en exégèse biblique." Pp. 35–53 in *Exégèse et herméneutique*. Ed. X. Léon-Dufour. Paris: Seuil.
1971b	"Sur l'exégèse de Genèse 1.1–2.4a." Pp. 67–84 in *Exégèse et herméneutique*. Ed. X. Léon-Dufour. Paris: Seuil.
1971c	"Esquisse de conclusion." Pp. 285–95 in *Exégèse et herméneutique*. Ed. X. Léon-Dufour. Paris: Seuil.
1971d	"Evénément et sens." Pp. 15–34 in *Révélation et histoire*. Paris: Aubier-Montaigne.
1971e	"Foreword." Pp. xiii–xvii in D. Ihde, *Hermeneutic Phenomenology*. Evanston, IL: Northwestern University Press.
1974a	*The Conflict of Interpretations*. Trans. D. Ihde. Evanston: Northwestern University Press.
1974b	"Manifestation et proclamation." Pp. 57–76 in *Le Sacré, Études et recherches*. Ed. E. Castelli. Paris: Aubier-Montaigne. ("Manifestation and Proclamation." *Journal of the Blaisdell Institute* 12 [1978] 13–35).
1974c	*Political and Social Essays*. Eds. D. Stewart and J. Bien. Athens: Ohio University Press.
1974d	"Philosophy and Religious Language." *The Journal of Religion* 54:71–85.
1975a	"Biblical Hermeneutics." *Semeia* 4:27–148.
1975b	"Introduction." Pp. 19–41 in *Les cultures et le temps*. Paris: Les Presses de l'UNESCO.
1975c	"Philosophical Hermeneutics and Theological Hermeneutics." "Ideology, Utopia, and Faith." Pp. 1–28 in *Protocol of the 17th Colloquy of the Center for*

Hermeneutical Studies. Ed. W. Wuellner. Berkeley, CA.

1975d   "Phenomenology and Hermeneutics." *Nous* 9:85–102.

1976a   "History and Hermeneutics." *The Journal of Philosophy.* 73:683–95.

1976b   *Interpretation Theory: Discourse and the Surplus of Meaning.* Fort Worth: Texas Christian University Press.

1976c   "Psychoanalysis and the Work of Art." *Psychiatry and the Humanities.* Ed. J. Smith. New Haven: Yale University Press.

1976d   "What is Dialectical?" *Freedom and Morality.* Ed. J. Bricke. Lawrence: University of Kansas Press.

1976e   "Ideology and Utopia as Cultural Imagination." *Philosophic Exchange* 2:17–28.

1976f   "What Is Dialectical." Pp. 173–89 in *Freedom and Morality.* Ed. J. Bricke. Lawrence: University of Kansas Press.

1977a   "Hermeneutic of the Idea of Revelation." Pp. 1–13 in *Protocol of the 27th Colloquy of the Center for Hermeneutical Studies.* Ed. W. Wuellner. Berkeley, CA.

1977b   *The Rule of Metaphor.* Trans. R. Czerny. Toronto: The University of Toronto Press.

1977c   "Toward a Hermeneutic of the Idea of Revelation." *Harvard Theological Review.* 70:1–37.

1977d   "Schleiermacher's Hermeneutics." *Monist* 60:181–97.

1977e   "Construing and Constructing: Review of E. D. Hirsch, *The Aims of Interpretation.*" Times Literary Supplement. Feb 25, p. 216.

1978a	"The Hermeneutical Function of Distanciation." Pp. 297-320 in *Exegesis*. Eds. F. Bovon and G. Rouiller. Pittsburgh: The Pickwick Press.
1978b	"My Relation to the History of Philosophy." *The Iliff Review*. November:5-12.
1978c	"The Metaphorical Process as Cognition, Imagination, and Feeling." *Critical Inquiry* 5:143-59.
1978d	"The Narrative Function." *Semeia* 13:177-202.
1978e	"Philosophical Hermeneutics and Biblical Hermeneutics." Pp. 321-39 in *Exegesis*. Ed. F. Bovon and G. Rouiller. Pittsburgh: The Pickwick Press.
1978f	*The Philosophy of Paul Ricoeur: An Anthology of His Work*. Eds. C. E. Reagan and D. Stewart. Boston: Beacon Press.
1978g	"The Task of Hermeneutics." Pp. 256-96 in *Exegesis*. Ed. F. Bovon and G. Rouiller. Pittsburgh: The Pickwick Press.
1978h	"Image and Language in Psychoanalysis." Pp. 293-324 in *Psychiatry and Language: Psychiatry and the Humanities* 3. Ed. J. H. Smith. New Haven, CT: Yale University Press.
1978i	"Imagination in Discourse and Action." Pp. 3-22 in *The Human Being in Action*. Ed. A.-T. Tymieniecka. Boston, MA: Reidel.
1979a	"Foreword." Pp. xvii-xxvi (Trans. David Pellauer) in André Lacocque, *The Book of Daniel*. Atlanta, GA: John Knox Press.
1979b	"The Logic of Jesus, the Logic of God." *Criterion* 18/2:4-6. (*Christianity and Crisis* 39/20:324-27).
1979c	"Naming God." Union Seminary Quarterly Review 34:215-27. (Trans. David Pellauer: "Nommer Dieu." *Études Théologiques et Religieuses* 52 [1977] 489-508.)

1979d "The Problem of the Foundation of Moral Philosophy." *Philosophy Today* 22:175-92.

1979e "Epilogue: The Sacred Text and the Community." Pp. 271-76 in *The Critical Study of Sacred Texts*. Ed. W. O'Flaherty. Berkeley Religious Studies Series. Los Angeles: University of California Press.

1979f "The Function of Fiction in Shaping Reality." *Man and World* 12:123-41.

1979g "The Hermeneutics of Testimony." *Anglican Theological Review* 61:435-61.

1979-80 "Response." *Biblical Research* 24/25:70-80.

1980a "The Bible and the Imagination." Paper presented at the William Rainey Harper Conference on Biblical Studies. The Divinity School, University of Chicago, October 4, 1979.

1980b "Narrative Time." Paper presented at the Conference on *Narrative: The Illusion of Sequence*. The University of Chicago Extension. To be published in a forthcoming issue of *Critical Inquiry*.

1980c "Narrative Theology." Paper presented at the Annual Meeting of the American Academy of Religion, New York, November, 1979.

SECONDARY SOURCES

Crossan, J. D., ed.
1975 *Semeia* 4: *Paul Ricoeur on Biblical Hermeneutics*.
1979-80 "Paradox Gives Rise to Metaphor: Paul Ricoeur's Hermeneutics and the Parables of Jesus." *Biblical Research* 24/25: 20-37.
1980 *Cliffs of Fall: Paradox and Polyvalence in the Parables of Jesus*. New York: Seabury Press (pp. 1-24 = Crossan, 1979-80).

Dornisch, L.
1974 *A Theological Interpretation of the Meaning of Symbol in the Theory of Paul Ricoeur*. Ann Arbor:

University Microfilms. (Paperback edition available.)

1975a   "Paul Ricoeur and Biblical Interpretation: A Selected Bibliography." *Semeia* 4:23–6.

1975b   "Symbolic Systems and the Interpretation of Scripture: An Introduction to the Work of Paul Ricoeur." *Semeia* 4:1–21.

Gerhart, M.
1976   "Paul Ricoeur, *La Métaphor vive*." *Religious Studies Review* 2:23–30.

Lacocque, A.
1979–80   "Job and the Symbolism of Evil." *Biblical Research* 24/25:7–19.

Lechner, R., ed.
1977   *Philosophy Today: A Presentation of the Rule of Metaphor by Paul Ricoeur*. Supplement to 21:4/4. Toronto: University of Toronto Press.

Mudge, L.
1979–80   "Paul Ricoeur on Biblical Interpretation." *Biblical Research* 24/25:38–69.

Perrin, N.
1976   *Jesus and the Language of the Kingdom*. Philadelphia, PA: Fortress Press.

Polzin, R.
1977   *Biblical Structuralism*. Philadelphia, PA: Fortress Press and Missoula: Scholars Press.

Polzin, R., & D. Robertson, eds.
1977   *Semeia* 7: Studies in the Book of Job.

Pope, M.
1965   *The Book of Job*. Garden City, NY: Doubleday.

Reagan, C., ed.
1979   *Studies in the Philosophy of Paul Ricoeur*. Athens: Ohio University Press.

ADDITIONAL BIBLIOGRAPHIES

Johnson, A.
1979   *A Bibliography of Semiological and Structural Studies of Religion*. Pittsburgh: Barbour Library, Pittsburgh

Theological Seminary. (Items 1380–1489 are works by Ricoeur.)

Revised and updated editions of bibliographies by Vansina and LaPointe (see *Semeia* 4 for references) are given in *Studies in the Philosophy of Paul Ricoeur*. Ed. C. Reagan. Athens: Ohio University Press, 1979.

I am also grateful to H. Frederick Reisz, Jr. and to David Pellauer for unpublished bibliographies of Ricoeur's works.

PART II
Essays on Paul Ricoeur and Job 38

JOB OR THE IMPOTENCE OF RELIGION AND PHILOSOPHY

André Lacocque
Chicago Theological Seminary

ABSTRACT

Chapter 38 of Job is approached through the dialectical method of explanation and interpretation (sense and reference) of a text-metaphor.

A definite emphasis is laid upon the use of various divine names in the Book, allowing the critical passage from the semiological "sameness" to the semantic referential level of "the difference." Discussed in this paper is the "as-if" stance of the author, a Jew projecting upon his main character Job a non-Israelite world-view. Such a "heuristic fiction" of the author himself takes off from the semiological code as used by Job's friends (*langue*) to the phenomenological relation subject-object of Job's problematic (*parole*), in the context of *Israel* functioning as sign-producing subject.

The book of *Job* is thus seen as a multileveled phenomenal encounter with suffering and evil, through various symbols, such as the use of different divine names, the foreign origin of the hero, the opacity of creation, etc., the hero becoming himself a symbol accepted and confirmed by God.

Such an apodictic confirmation of the most fragile and unstable "man in question" opens up an ontological understanding of God and man. The starting point—which Job discovers only at the very end—is the hermeneutic circle of faith and understanding leading to a "second naiveté" which is symbolically expressed in the book as a re-stitution.

SECTION I
WAYS OF VIEWING THE TEXT OF JOB 38-42

As such, Job's questioning of God's justice is clear. It is not raised here for the first time in the Bible, although for the first time with such a powerful, overwhelming, uncomproming insistence. This point is important, for it makes both the so-called "response" of God to Job, and the subsequent hero's submission to God all the more unexpected and properly incomprehensible. For it seems undeniable that *Yhwh* badly misses the target. The lesson He teaches to the agonizing man appears to be: "Don't ask questions! Suffer in silence! Who are you to speak to Me? Look around at the majesty of My creation and know once for all that you are incompetent. Your agony is trivial, your questions are meaningless, your quest is vain."

Such a solution of the tension entertained by the plot may satisfy Job's "friends" of then and now. That it convinces Job himself is unbelievable. True, the texts are explicit: Job repents, he cancels his former words, he lays his hand upon his mouth and is unable to answer (42:6; 40:4,5). But one can wonder what Job found so decisive in God's words. The embarrassment of the critics is eloquent. Marvin Pope speaks of "the seemingly magnificent irrelevance of much of the content of the divine speeches" (lxxxi). For Yehezkel Kaufmann, "Job's special case is not dealt with. The foundations of the moral universe are at stake . . . the special plight of Job falls into the background" (337). Adolphe Lods recalls that Job had in advance rejected any demonstration of force without proof of justice (9:2,3,14-16,17, 20,29-31; 10:6,7; 13:15-21). Lods concludes that chapters 38-42 advocate a "resigned agnosticism" (679).

In what follows, however, I shall propose another reading of Job's confrontation with the theophany. For doing so, I propose that we devote ourselves to a double reflection. A reflection upon the nature of the document we find in Job 38-42, and a reflection upon a hermeneutical approach to such a text.

1. Nature of the Text's Final Chapter

One of the problems of the book of Job, from a critical point of view, is constituted by its narrative framework. Today critics recognize in it a popular tale about an individual hero by the name of Job, a saga which the author reworked for his own purpose, making of it the indispensable inner referent of the dialogical central part of the book. In fact, this piece in a popular vein specifies *the* issue dealt with and gives the tone to the whole document: "*Is it for nought that Job fears God?*" (1:9).

This insidious question is raised by the Satan (the prosecutor; the "Qategor" of Rabbinic literature). It challenges not only Job or the theologian of today, but God Himself. In advance, all responses arguing that there is some advantage in being pious are rejected, they would short-change the issue. Since Job's "friends" overlook or reject this principle, their arguments amount to a pious lie (cf. 13:4-11; 8:5-7, 20-22; 11:13-19; 22:21-28; alternatively in the mouth of Bildad, Tsophar and Eliphaz). And as for the cries of Job demanding some acknowledgment of his virtues, in the name of the retributive justice principle, they only worsen his wounds, like the potsherd with which he scrapes himself among the ashes (2:8). This, however, remains: Job knows that he is innocent of any crime and that his suffering is undeserved. It is thus forbidden from the outset to get rid of him and of his existential problem through a theological formula applied to his "case."

But, if all religious response is deemed incapable of taking us out of the impasse, is there any valid solution to the problem of innocent suffering? Meeting the challenge, the last chapters of the book present a theophany. By means of a long two-part discourse, God succeeds — to the surprise of the modern reader, more reluctant, or perhaps less insightful than the hero — in convincing Job (38:1-42:6; cf. 40:3-5; 42:2-6). But how could a God-guided visit to a zoo untie the Jobian knot? How could one draw consolation from one's demonstrated incapacity to steer the cosmic ship? Exegetes of the book of Job have therefore sometimes concluded, from the irrelevance of Yhwh's response, that the theophany itself, not the accompanying discourses, is the decisive factor.

This opinion, as we will see, is not too far from the truth /1/, but remains a sheer *petitio principii* as long as it is not buttressed by a whole series of elements indispensable for the understanding of Job's message. I do not forget that we are dealing here with the final chapters only, but, as M. Pope wrote (lxxiv): "Either the book ends in magnificent anticlimax, or we must see the highlight is the divine speeches."

2. God and Creation

Chapters 38-42 start with these far-reaching introductory words: "Then *Yhwh* responded to Job from the midst of the whirlwind." There is a decisive element in the book of Job which the critics do not generally take seriously enough: Job is not an Israelite, he comes from "the land of Uz," somewhere between Arabia and Idumeia (1:1). "He was the greatest of all the children of the East" (1:3). Likewise, his so-called friends also come from regions in the same vicinity. Eliphaz is from Theyman, Bildad from Shuach, Tsophar from Naamah (2:11) /2/.

It is therefore fitting that they refer to God solely as *Eloah*, *El Shaddy*, *Elohim* /3/. By that means, the author makes clear that his heroes' beliefs have reached perhaps the greatest refinement in the non-Israelite *religious* quest of man. The tale acknowledges this as a remarkable achievement on the part of the wisest among the Gentiles. Job himself shares the same religious tenets and, although in radical opposition with his colleagues' conclusions, he cannot help being himself sucked deeper and deeper into the quicksand of his friends' problematic. Many critics have noticed the fact that in his entire protest, Job continues to believe that a divine recompense must sanction man's virtue in this world (see, e.g., Sellin-Fohrer: 332). The problem of Job remains without solution precisely because it creates a situation without issue. It is so because, as we shall see, it takes for granted that justice is a constitutive element of the cosmic order.

The break-through in Job's stalemate is wrought, not by *El*, *Eloah*, *El Shadday*, *Elohim*, but by *Yhwh*; not by the god of religion and philosophy, "the god of philosophers and scholars" (Pascal), but by the God of the Covenant, the God of Israel. Hence, the problematic leaves the realm of "religious" speculation to enter the properly Israelite *Weltanschauung*. Only then do Job and his companions find a way out of the impasse wherein their religious ideas (or: natural theology) had locked them. For, in point of fact—Job now learns it from the mouth of the One who flatly denies the truth of individual retribution (cf. 42:7 "*lō nekhonah*")—there is in the universe no retribution of any kind. Within the limits of chapter 38, we already learn that the sun shines on the just and the wicked (38:12–15) and the rare and precious rain falls to no purpose on the deserts (38:25–27). One must bow to the facts: the practice of justice has no foundation in the cosmic order. The just finds no "recompense" for his justice in the balance of natural phenomena. Piety is purely rewardless, or it simply does not exist.

True, creation is good news, "the sons of God shouted for joy" (38:7); but Job not only was not present among them, he even does not seem to have any share in it: "Where were you?" asks God (38:4). That's the question. Where is man in all that? True, he appears soon enough in the picture but, ominously, under the form of the wicked (38:13)! Dawn reveals the wicked's crimes perpetrated under the cover of the night. What this means on the universal scale is that there are "cracks" in God's good creation! The cosmic laws—the breaking of dawn every morning—are gracious, but in a sort of negative way; they set a limit to crimes in the world. Besides, as norms, they are applied almost mechanically, as clay is changed under the seal (38:14). *Ethic is absent from the picture.*

The display of God's works continues along the same pattern. Job 38:16 takes us on an awesome trip to the depth of the abyss, to "the gates of death" (38:17). The least one can say is that there is not romanticism here about nature. True, the first creation is light, as in Genesis 1:3, but it is immediately followed by darkness, and one is not more contingent than the other (38:19). The same dark side is always parallel with the bright one. Snow and hail are "treasures" (38:22), but they are inanimate, soulless. They are even weapons against men (38:23; cf. Josh. 10:11; Isa. 30:30; cf. Sir 39:29 "in His storehouse, kept for the proper time, are fire, hail, famine, disease.")

Whereas the philosophy of nature of Ben Sira, for instance, is positive, Job questions such an optimism. In 38:25-27 God speaks of "waterflood, lightning, thunder." They recall the whirlwind of 38:1. Now, thunder-showers can be a blessing, especially in the Middle-East, but where is the blessing, when the rain falls "*'al 'eretz lō' 'ish, midbar lō 'adam bō'*" (38:26)? It just "saturates the barren barrenness and causes grass, where it can grow, to spring forth" (38:27). The fact is that rain has no "father," dew has no "begetter"; they are not motivated, nobody directs them (38:28). They are not "acted" by any agent with a purpose. There is here no parallel to the Ugaritic goddess Pidray. The same is true about ice or hoar-frost, etc. (38:29-32). The readers are thus witnessing a thorough demythologization of Nature. Not only are things following once-for-all set laws, but man has no control (not even magical) upon cosmic forces. Moreover, there is no response in them to man's prayer and suffering (38:33-34). The "rules of heaven" are without feeling. They have no regard for man (38:35).

3. The Shift in Divine Names

But another element adds itself to the already rich variations on the theme of the divine names. *Yhwh* speaks to Job about the creation by *Elohim* (38:7), *El* (38:41; 40:9,19), *Eloah* (39:17; 40:2), *Shadday* (40:2), but never of the creation by *Yhwh*. In other words, if creation is the work of a non-personalized divinity, it becomes clear why it lacks ethical standards, i.e., norms to facilitate interpersonal relationships. Job therefore was wrong from the start in attempting to bring *El*, *Eloah*, *El Shadday*, i.e., the "wholly other," in judgment for it. Only *Yhwh*, the covenantal God *of Israel* makes himself near to men. His transcendence does not mean "separation from," but "separation for" /4/; it expresses the total commitment of the Creator to His creation.

The shift from "*El*" to "*Yhwh*"—from cosmic deity to the God acting in human affairs—is in fact the qualitatively infinite jump from nature-bound religious belief to history-making covenantal faith. All religious systems are by necessity in the image of Bildad's, Tsophar's, and Eliphaz's theological constructions. But the final theophany in the book of Job renders obsolete all theological systems, for their sole *raison d'être* was to make the Vision possible. When this happens, however—"now my eyes have seen you" (42:5)—it is revealed to all that the Vision was from the beginning an explosive material cast in the religious mold provided by the nations (cf. 40:4–5), for instance categories of Edomite wisdom (cf. 1:1, 3; 2:11). The faith Event finds its home in the religious Institution, but, in its turn, ceaselessly transfigures it into Event.

The "explosive material" is called by different names in Israel's Scriptures. One of the designations of God's transforming power, e.g., is "justice," a common enough term. But, in Israel's conception, justice has not been woven into the fabric of the universe. Only through misunderstanding would one see such an idea implied in the "goodness" of creation. *Tōb* means "capable of fulfilling one's vocation; capable of meeting the Creator's design." The universe is *tōb* because created as the framework of human response to divine entreaty. That is why creation presents no inherent warrant for its ultimate success. *Bereshit Rabba* 9:4 has the Creator exclaiming: *Haway sheya 'amod*, may it endure! André Neher writes: "From the outset . . . history is stamped with a sign of *radical insecurity*" (1968:142). It is the price to pay for a world that is not static but in process of becoming *tōb*, i.e., fitting God's intention in creating it in the first place. From the beginning, man (Adam) is called to "make justice" /5/ in the world (cf. Mic 6:8), that is, to engage in a *relationship* with the Creator. Inspired by a totally original conception, Israel does not invite man to bow before an ideal justice, outside of him, but to realize justice in the framework of the eventful I-Thou dialogue /6/.

From this perspective it becomes clear that God's exposition (Job 38–42) is not just a display of power. And it could not be, because of incontrovertible reasons which no critics of Job could miss, but which they thought had been suddenly abandoned by the author in the last chapters of the book. First, as if to cut away any modern misunderstandings (but they dodge the obstacle all the same), Job had responded in advance to the futility of God's "showoff": "Am I a sea, or a sea monster, that you get a watch over me?" (7:12). The second motive is decisive. If, as a matter of fact, *Yhwh's* discourses were a mere demonstration of omnipotence, they would indeed vindicate the stance of Job's friends who praised the arbitrary power of the Divine /7/. Then the book as a whole is self-defeating, an exercise in futility. One then does not understand how in the world the author can put in the mouth of *Yhwh*: "My wrath is kindled against you (Eliphaz) and against your two companions because you did not speak to Me *nekhonah*, as did My servant Job" (42:7). We are in a total hermeneutical impasse, because we have gone astray, lured as we were by a fiction pretending "to be plain and trivial" (Ricoeur, 1975:98) while sending the reader to a referent (cf. below, section II). In fact, the magnificence of God's painting throws dust in the eyes, as it were /8/. It conceals a terrible drama: so much power, wisdom, care, might well end up in nothingness! For, as there is no Thou without I, neither is there I without Thou. "Where were you (Job) when I laid the foundations of the earth?" (38:4a). Where are you now? (cf. Gen 3:9). The only possible answer is that Job and all of the suffering humanity are in the whirlwind. And who, being in the fiery furnace built by nature or by Nebuchadnezzar, would not look for God's presence *outside* of it, and preferably in the aloofness and the motionlessness of the heavens /9/? But *Yhwh* is Himself in the whirlwind, nowhere else. Job had shouted: "Where are you, God?" God now returns the question to Job: "I am here, in the midst of the tempest, as I was in the burning bush, and in the crematory oven with Shadrack, Meshak and Abed-Nego, but you, Job, are you still with Me?"

4. The God of Nature and the God of History

Job "lays his hands upon his mouth" (40:4; cf. 42:2–6) for he realizes that the injustice he underwent had first made another victim in the person of God Himself. "Therefore I reject (my words)." Writes L. J. Kuyper, "Job now discerns his folly in employing words of arguments within a moralistic, reward-retribution framework. These words he now rejects as worthless and repents of his folly in using them 'therefore I reject (my words), and I repent in dust and ashes.'" (Kuyper: 94). These last terms especially are remarkable. According to the Prologue, Job had been reduced to sitting "among the ashes" (2:8). He now *chooses* to be "in dust and ashes" (42:6)! In the most touching move of the whole book, Job rejects (*ma'as*) all attempts at confirming right and respectability /10/. He is no longer impatient to leave the heap of ashes where he sits.

But Job's repentance is not caused by a last-minute realization that he has sinned against justice. Job is not at this point less innocent than he was at the beginning. When his friends tried to demonstrate that he deserved suffering as the right punishment of his sins, they were wrong then and they are still wrong now (42:7–9) /11/. Job's *nehama* (repentance) is yielded by his wisdom, not by any feeling of culpability: "I had heard of You by hearsay, but now my eyes see you" (42:5). Rather than having discovered something about himself (a hidden iniquity perhaps), Job has discovered something about God: that He did not remain untouched during Job's torture. He had bet on Job (1:12), thus putting Himself and His creation at stake. He had admitted to being radically questioned in the person of his human *vis-à-vis*. The question from the beginning had been: either the covenantal God is affirmed (sense of the word-root "amen," "emunah" = faith) through man's gratuitous response to His gratuitous love; or else God has annihilated Himself in committing the whole of His being on an unworthy and deceitful *hêbêl* (vanity). Job holds in his hands God's vindication or defeat.

It has been said that there is a tragic dimension to Job /12/. Already Theodore of Mopsuestia saw in the book an imitation of Greek tragedy /13/. Such a judgment is based on a misreading of chapters 38–42. Greek tragedy may not be absent from the book of Job, *but then it is present as an enemy*. Job is precisely the protest against a "Platonic" or tragic concept of "the divine, unalterable, 'total world order'" /14/ which had reached Palestine during the Hellenistic period and probably even before. Job is to be put in the same category of books as the later Qoheleth. It is an individual criticism of the doctrine of retribution. "Its conclusion is neither resignation nor Promethean defiance, nor even a change in God from arbitrariness to righteousness" /15/.

True, the modern reader is fooled by the apocryphal speech of Elihu (chapters 32–37)—on a par with the second epilogue in Qoheleth 12:12–14—which attempts to bridge the radical criticism of the book with the reactionary wisdom of a Ben Sira who about 180 BCE proclaimed again the doctrine of retribution in all its massiveness /16/. Such additions only demonstrate how unpopular and scandalous Job and Qoheleth appeared to their contemporaries and to the following generations (up until today, one may say). But in twisting the message of their masters, those "bourgeois" disciples asepticized the original author's problem: *mah yitrōn?*, *ha-leḥinam?* "Who ever came before me with a gift that I should repay?" /17/.

According to the retribution-principle, man's justice is repaid. It is rewarded, recompensed. It causes beneficial effects in nature. For the natural and the ethical are here intertwined. To be ethical is to be natural. A moral person is one attuned to cosmic forces. But "in Hebrew religion—and in Hebrew religion alone—the ancient bond between man and nature is broken. Those who served *Yhwh* must forgo the richness, the fulfillment, the consolation of life which moves in tune with great rhythms and sky ... Man remained outside of nature ... never sharing its mysterious life, never an actor in the perennial cosmic pageant in which the sun is made 'to rise on the evil and on the good' and the rain is sent 'on the just and unjust.'" (Frankfort, 1948:343–44).

Nature is not beyond Israel's concern, however, but in the words of G. von Rad, "the *natural* orders, fixed by God's word, mysteriously guarantee a world in which in his own time God's *historical* saving activity will begin" /18/. In the book of Job the passage from one realm to another is expressed in the shift from *El, Eloah, Shadday,* to *Yhwh*. As I insisted earlier, Job is not an Israelite /19/. "Natural theology" gives a *religious* feeling for the Divine. So Job's author finds no difficulty in stating that *Eloah's* work in the universe is known even by animals. But to that effect, there is no need for any other bond with the Divine than the one established by the creation. No personal, ethical, covenant is necessary; "ask now the beasts (*Behemoth*!), and they shall teach you, the fowls in the sky, and they shall tell you," etc. (12:7-12). Nature catches a faint echo of God's "ways" and "mighty deeds." Job 26:7-14 says this plainly. In fact, strictly speaking, only non-Israelites are religious, for Israel is anti-religious, as she is anti-natural. Religion leads to an impasse. *El* is indifferent. Nature is bound to operate according to a once-for-all set of causes and effects /20/. As such, it is true, chaos is kept in check and God's grace is truly at work. But no intimate covenantal relationship between God and man is expressed this way. So far, Job's suffering or man's existential quest is irrelevant. Man is on earth while God dwells in heavens. As long as Job and his "friends" try to relate to such an *El* (cf. 31:2; 22:12-14; 25:2; in God's speeches about *El*: 38:1-40:2; 40:6-41:34), there is no response to their query.

For the responding God is the God who shares with man in his pathos (cf. Abraham Heschel's work). Only *Yhwh* can respond to Job, because He is involved in the suffering of man. But then one leaves the certitude of astral regularity and the comfort of cause-effect determinism. In becoming *Yhwh* (the God of Israel), *El* (the God of religion) has left omnipotence and chosen dependence /21/. Job lays his hand on his mouth. Now that he has been confronted by *Yhwh*, he knows that he was calling to account the prime victim of history. *Yhwh needed* to be vindicated by Job: He had bet on him, He had put his faith in him (Prologue). "Is it for nought that Job fears God?" asked the Satan. The wager of God was that it was for nought. Job, at the end, repents for having expected a reward for his righteousness. In the relationship with *Yhwh*, justice, like love, is not in need of any recompense, it is its own reward /22/. Justice is both the beginning and the end of the project of the two-who-become-one. Therefore, Daniel's three companions, about to be thrown into the crematorium, testify to their gratuitous and indefectible fidelity to the Living God: "If our God whom we serve is able to deliver us from the burning fiery furnace, He'll deliver us. If not, be it known to you O king, that we will not serve your gods or worship the golden image you have set up" (Dan 3:17-18). And Job, bringing Israel's faith to its highest crest, exclaims: "Though He slay me, yet I trust in Him" (13:15, Qere).

> Alas, rejoins Rabbi Eleazar, I see now that I address my requests to Someone who does not possess anything /23/.

SECTION II
REFLECTION UPON THE INTERPRETATIONS OF JOB 38-42

The aim of this second part is to reflect upon what we have done in Section I. What have been the leading principles of our hermeneutical approach? Logically, I realize, one could question the order of these divisions. Practically, however, one first interprets (e.g., the current discourse), then one reflects upon the ontology and the method of interpretation. First, one thinks and speaks, then one brings those existential (and existentiell) acts to consciousness in order to examine what has gone on and whether the hermeneutics is correct.

1. Summary

Let us first summarize our findings. Over against the principle of retributive justice, Job proclaims his innocence of any misdeed or misbehavior (cf. Job 31). For if his suffering is construed as a chastisement, then it punishes man for just being a man! It is man's nature which would be blamed upon man by the very One who gave him such a nature. If someone is to be punished, it is not man but God. There is no justice in Him.

The "friends" have a strictly *religious* stance and Job demonstrates that they are in an impasse. Job's stance is strictly *philosophical* and he locks himself in another impasse. The book of Job is about the impotence of religion and philosophy. The religious principle of distributive justice cannot be maintained, and it is necessary to transcend Hume's statement according to which either God is powerful but unwilling to save, hence He is not good, or God is willing to save but incapable, hence He is impotent /24/.

In responding to Job, *Yhwh* starts by showing that man is inserted into nature. Nature is controlled by *El* granting it a set of rules which are not the only possible ones, as they are not intrinsic but external to nature, and neither are they logical, mythological, or ethical. Man thus is plunged into the irrational and the amoral.

The conclusion would thus be, after Ad. Lods, a "resigned agnosticism," were it not for the fact that it is *Yhwh* who speaks of *El*'s works. Consequently, we leave the level of religion or philosophy for the one of the existential I-Thou relationship where both partners of the covenant are affected by events lived in common. Their exchange is based on mutuality, so that if Job must serve God "for nought," it is because God first of all creates the world "for nought." True, on the basis of Ps. 104:31 Calvin writes: "Status mundi in Dei laetitia fundatus est"; but precisely God's joy is in the gratuity of creation. God's action is beyond the law of compensation. God is good without expectation of retribution for his goodness; he favors both the righteous and the wicked (Luke 6:35)! That is why, in return, Job is expected to love without recompense for his love (a contradiction in terms).

Thus, Robert M. Polzin is wrong when he contrasts the presence of the question "What Job?" to an alleged lack of question "What God?" in our book. *The* question of Job is precisely "What

God?" through the mediation of the question "What Job?" the multiplicity of God's names is readily indicative of the fact (*Elohim* is used 3 times, *Shadday* 31 times, *Eloah* 41 times, *El* 55 times, according to R. Pfeiffer). Because he overlooked this central element, Polzin can also oppose (113) the unknown "Job" introduced in 1:1 /25/ to *El* etc., "one who does not need to be defined . . . (although) He possesses six different names" /26/. But then the very structure of the book becomes self-contradictory. Job acknowledges that he was wrong, but God, who brought Job to such a confession, declares that Job was right (42:7). This, says Polzin, is "the most amazing inconsistency in the whole book" (60). "Job is led to the implicit denial of the theophantic speeches of 38–41 which had in effect condemned his previous position" (71). (*Sic!*).

Structural analysis can be applied successfully only to closed, "dead" systems, because it subordinates *parole* to language. In Section I, we have proceeded differently, for even the reading of Job with the eyes of the "first naiveté" reveals how little a closed system the book is. Even Polzin must acknowledge that "if Job vacillates through the course of the story, so does God" (106). The story evolves in a train of oppositions; even "God's position changes radically throughout the story" (107).

2. A Restorative Hermeneutics

"Any text interpretation implies by necessity a break from the text. But in the very break happens the encounter. Hermeneutical dialogue aims at filling the difference which gives birth to it . . . Fidelity to the spirit always seems a treason of the letter" (Resweber: 71, 72). The real problem is not so much to know what a text says as to fathom what it does not say. This, says Heidegger, "is the soul of dialogue. It brings those who speak into the beyond of all words" (1959:171).

Inspired by this conception, our applied hermeneutics in Section I has been "restorative" or "reflective," in the words of Paul Ricoeur. It recognizes the importance of a controlling symbol (or set of symbols), also called "qualifier," (e.g., Israel). Here, it is suggested that the control is provided by the understanding of God as God of history in contradistinction to the nature-bound divinities of "religion." In other words, the text of Job appears already as interpretation by the author, awaiting another interpretation by the reader. Job 38–42 is a variation on the theme *Yhwh*, a metaphorical interpretation of the names of God with their particular references, inserted in a literary frame which itself is metaphorical.

Here is therefore a privileged case in point where one has to pass over from a rhetoric of the word to a semantic of discourse (cf. Ricoeur, 1975:75). Job 38–42 introduces a strong tension between the terms at face value, and what they actually state: the metaphorical character is not so much at the level of discrete expressions as it is at the level of the whole discourse. It regards "the very functioning of predication at the level of the whole statement," and discovers that "the strategy of discourse by which the metaphorical statement obtains its meaning is absurdity" (1975:77). The literal interpretation is destroyed internally by this "semantic impertinence" skillfully introduced by the fact that *Yhwh* speaks of *El*'s creation! Thus, the *meaning* (the objective qualities) of the discourse must be reconciled with its *reference* (i.e., the "what" with the "that about which").

In the context of the opposition of Ricoeur to Roman Jakobson and others on the point that poetic language would be "self-contained" (Northrup Frye), i.e., without reference to reality, it is clear that Job provides a reinterpretation of reality "in spite of, and thanks to, the abolition of the reference which corresponds to the literal interpretation of the statement," by means, that is, of "a second-order reference" (1975:84). For, although the Job text seems to show a world out there, as does a descriptive or didactic language, another level of reality is uncovered which corresponds to the Heideggerian non-manipulable being-in-the-world. It "*redescribes*" reality "by the twisting pathway of heuristic fiction" (Ricoeur, 1975:88).

The *qualifier* is contained in the Name *Yhwh*, while the *ultimate referent* is "human experience centered around the *limit-experiences* [Job's] which would correspond to the *limit-expressions* of religious discourse [Cf. here Job's repentance]" (Ricoeur, 1975:34; cf. Jaspers's "boundary experiences").

But are we entitled to call the text metaphoric? What are the signs of metaphoricity? Ricoeur answers that they are to be found "in the plot (in Via's sense), in the challenge which this plot displays for the main characters, and in the answer of those characters [here Job and secondarily his 'friends'] to the crisis situation [here the catharsis brought about by *Yhwh's* discourse]" (97).

Now it can be said that the final divine discourse is a metaphoric plot inserted into a larger metaphoric plot, *viz.* the whole book of Job. That is exactly the function of the prologue of the book, which also takes the dialogues from one level to another, i.e., from the level of wisdom dialogical contest to the level of wisdom poetry in a popular tale. All in the book is striving towards the *dénouement* and must be read accordingly from a wholistic approach. It is indeed easy to transpose Crossan's words to fit our problem: "if (the parable's) normalcy was not symbolic, the telling of the story [here, the divine discourse] would be pointless" (cited by Ricoeur, 1975:98). Pointless is exactly how Job 38–42 appeared to many of its interpreters! The Jobian declaration: "I knew you from hearsay, but now my eyes saw you!" /27/ should, however, be taken as an incontrovertible clue that one must pass over from "hearsay," to its referent, the "eyesight." And Ricoeur adds: "The parable should be interpreted metaphorically *because* it pretends to be plain and trivial" (1975:98) whereas it may "be converted into a proverb or an eschatological saying" (102). Such a convertibility to proverbial expression is for Ricoeur a clear sign of the parabolic character of the discourse. Along that line, my contention is that the name *Yhwh* plays in Job 38–42 the same role as, e.g., the notion of "Kingdom of God" in Jesus' gospel. It is a "limit-expression by virtue of which the different forms of discourse employed by religious language are 'modified'" (1975:98). It contains the Ramseyan "qualifier" which "forces us to rework . . . all our experience" (120) of God. Then, the "qualifier" is not, as so many critics believed, just "completing" the language of Job's on the divine (*El*, *Eloah*, *Elohim*, *El Shadday*) but it constitutes the point of rupture of the paradox: it re-orients by disorienting.

Now, with the Tetragrammaton as key to the Jobian text, we are decisively on the level of language. Its meaning is a discourse and its revelation is a "parole." Therefore "*Yhwh* spoke to Job from the whirlwind" is the appropriate mode of resolving the tension at the basis of the whole book. The resolution *is* in the speaking of God who utters His Name and focuses Job's attention on the Speaker Himself. There is therefore a "substantial existence" to the Tetragrammaton sign before it is involved, e.g., by the book of Job, in a differential system of signs (here: *El*, *Eloah*, etc.). This prevents the issue from being a closed semiotic system. Using the Tetragrammaton is a performative act.

3. Eidetic Reduction

Is it purely coincidental if, in the tale, Job is stripped of his possessions, and ultimately of his dear ones and of his Shalom, in a move corresponding to the eidetic reduction of phenomenology? Is not on the contrary that abstraction of the world of Job, that laying bare of all structures, the very condition for the rising of a new ontology of God and man? Now the order of these last words is decisive: man's ontology depends upon God's. That is why in the epiphany of the last chapters of the book the accent is not on Job's but on God's being. And, as far as Job is concerned, the point of the parable is less the Job of before and the Job of after, than the Job in process from "religion" to intimate relationship (covenant) with that God whose name is *Yhwh*. The passage from the former to the latter is brought about by God's demonstration that there is no ethical dimension in the natural realm, only in the societal. Hence, Job as first man must witness the ethical emptiness of the universe, a stage set *for an act to happen*, but not the act itself. When Job enacts the passage to covenantal relationship, he forthwith reaches the very peak of the experience. Job 42 makes clear that he is not the first man anymore, but the suffering servant as depicted in Isaiah 53, a chapter starting with the words "to whom has the arm of *YHWH* been uncovered?" Only in the framework of covenant with *YHWH* is a vicarious suffering of the servant conceivable. No pain or grief is ever vicarious or substitutive by itself or in itself; but the relational ties binding God and His people do indeed make one out of two. Here the substitution becomes central, God taking the stand of man for man, man taking the stand of God for God (cf. Exod 3:14–15; 7:1). For what nature is incapable of doing, love which transcends nature is able to do /28/.

Polzin readily insists upon the book of Job being "a dialectical working out of a series of contradictions" (72). He is right, and, one must add, the shifts are not from one Gestalt to another Gestalt (in which case it would be incorrect to speak of eidetic reduction). For, on the one hand, the rich, blessed Job *was* the poor, wretched (but *not cursed*) Job. His riches concealed this fundamental vulnerability and frailty (as the subsequent events prove). And, on the other hand, the wretched Job, led into temptation by wife and friends *was* already victorious and "restored." His final restoration was his entering the Shalom for the first time without ambivalence!

In the meantime, *Yhwh* has spoken. According to Martin Heidegger, the very condition for a word to be is the death of the speaker. True, there is an essential difference between the human language which expresses Being in betraying it, and the Word of the Being itself; but in both cases speaking puts the subject in a position of exteriority and thus bespeaks the speaker's frailty and vulnerability. Thus, the final discourse of the book of Job is perhaps not only a process of demythologization and de-moralization of nature, but also of what Heidegger after Max Weber and others, calls dedivinization (Entgötterung). It is indicated to Job that the images created by our *eros* or our *eidos* are idols. To the silence of God may only correspond silence about God ("Job put his hand on his mouth . . . ").

In anguish, we discover the total collapse of meaning. As J. P. Resweber puts it: "As we are unable . . . to catch on to any existent, we discover our primal condition of being-to-the-world" (98). But, if the existent is elusive, the Being Himself, so proclaims Israel, comes near to us and speaks, "from the midst of the whirlwind."

NOTES

/1/ Y. Kaufmann's stance is that the supreme argument in those chapters is God's manifestation, not what he says. For Kuhl (*ThR* 1953, 1954) the original book of Job ended without any kind of God's speech, but with the revelation of God in the thunderstorm. (Cited by Eissfeldt: 460).

/2/ In general, the Jewish traditional literature has been more sensitive to this fact. According to *Deut. R.* 2.4 (cf. *Gen. R.* 57.4), Job was the most pious Gentile that ever lived. Indeed he was the only pious Canaanite living at the time of the Exodus (*BB* 15a-15b, although the same text recognizes that most Rabbis thought of him as a Jew, cf. R. Johannan, for example). He was uncircumcized and not even a proselyte (*Gen. R.* 80.4; 73.9); a prophet of the Gentiles (*Sed. Eliahu R.* 18, 141-147; *Sed. Eliahu Z.* 10-11, 191-192; *Yelam. in Yalkut* I, 766). He was king of Edom (*Gen. R.* 83.8) whereas Eliphaz was king of Theyman and a son of Esau (*Tanh. B* I, 166; Tg. Jerus. Gen. 36.12. For the LXX, Job's friends were princes of Edom, cf. Louis Ginzberg, *Legends*, V, 387, n. 31). A Borayta to *BB* 15b stresses that Job was a non-Jew, so that the problem of the book centers around that "gentility" of Job.

/3/ The only exceptions are readily justifiable, they are citations of well-known aphorisms: 12:9 and 28:28 (the latter is a gloss according to Dhorme). Moreover in 12:9, the intention of the text may be to emphasize the originality of Israel's God in contradistinction to the pagan divinities mentioned in v. 6, unless we adopt with M. Pope (*ad loc.*) the text of several MSS which read "*Eloah*" here. The reading in "*Yhwh*" may have been done late to conform with Isa 41.20.

/4/ Cf. Norman Snaith: 30.

/5/ As also to "make the truth," cf. Ezek 18:9; Neh 9:33; Tob 4:6; 13:6; IQS I, 5, 6; John 3:21; 2 Clem 31:2; etc.

/6/ As a corollary, sins exist only in the same framework (cf. Rom 5:13). The more the relation with God is intimate, the more serious is sin and its divine sentence, cf. Amos 3:2. No nation, however, finds itself outside of the Noahide Berith and thus devoid of responsibility.

/7/ Cf. 5:8-16; 9:4-10; 11:7-11; 12:9-25; 22:12-14; 26:5-13.

/8/ Cf. M. Buber: "The Living God is not only a self-revealing God, but also a self-concealing God." Cited by E. L. Fackenheim (Friedlander: 511).

/9/ Spatial dualism pervades the book of Job. Job conceives of God as dwelling in heavens, as his friends do, cf. 31:2 (and 22:12-14; 25:2).

/10/ One of the possible meanings of the term *kabōd* is honor, that respectability Job was so anxious to protect throughout his discourses (cf. 19:9; 29:20).

/11/ As Roland de Pury puts it: Had Job "repented because of his ill fortune, it would mean that he did serve God in order to be happy" (19). Cf. 12:6.

/12/ Cf. for example Paul Ricoeur, *La Symbolique du Ma* , especially page 299, where Ricoeur sees the response of Job in the last chapters as a submission to the *tragic*, for he converts freedom and necessity into fate, thus triumphing over the ethical vision of the world.

/13/ Cf. Louis Pirot (131-134). Some modern authors concur. Kallen (19-21) sees the influence of Euripides. Others think rather of Aeschylus; etc.

/14/ Cf. Martin Hengel (125).

/15/ Martin Hengel (109). Let us also cite this significant misunderstanding of G. von Rad in stating the inferiority of Job in comparison with the Servant of II Isaiah: "the God with whom Job is struggling should first have become another God. He should have utterly been transformed." G. von Rad so misses the point that he indiscriminately uses "*Yhwh*" at places where "*El(ohim)*" is in the text (cf. *Wisdom in Israel*: 211, 221, etc.)

/16/ The Rabbis did not fall into the trap. For R. Akiba, e.g., Elihu is identical with Balaam (j. Sotah 5, 20d). According to *Test. of Job* 7-9, Elihu was inspired by Satan and deserved, still more so than the other "friends," to be destroyed by God. At one point, Eliphaz is said to have announced Elihu's damnation.

/17/ Translation of M. Pope *ad* 41:11.

/18/ Cf. von Rad's commentary on the Noahide Covenant (1972b:134).

/19/ Among modern critics, Robert Pfeiffer (660) has been particularly sensitive to this crucial element. He calls attention to the fact that there is in the book of Job no reference to Israel, its land, history, culture, and religion (678). The practices are those in force among all ancient civilized nations. Already Ernest Renan had written (in 1894): there is in Job "nothing particularly Hebraic." But Pfeiffer is wrong when he believes that the book was written by an Edomite (683).

/20/ I want to stress that it is *one* set of natural rules among other possible sets, as Gen 1 shows. For, according to Israel, the natural laws are not intrinsic but external. "Natural" does not mean "logical." There is nothing logical in the law of gravity; the astronauts are not going into the illogical, but into other sets of laws. Job is made witness of such a set which happens to be the one of our human earth. But if there is here no logic, there is also no human control upon the laws of nature. That is why the divine questions to Job are merely rhetorical. Can you? Of course he cannot. The demonstration is thus first negative: Job (as Primal Man, i.e., as representative of all men) is in a world foreign to him. It does not belong to his logic and still less to his ethic. Cf. André Lacocque (1978).

/21/ Cf. Schelling: "All of history is virtually an enigma without a concept of an agonizing God." (In the German original, p. 403).

/22/ "Whoso loveth God truly must not expect to be loved by Him in return," wrote Spinoza. This saying is not unequivocal. Rollo May, however, comments, "The love of God is its own reward, that beauty and truth are to be loved because they are good, and not because they will redound to the credit of the artist or scientist or philosopher, who loves them" (204).

/23/ *Taanit* 28a, cited by André Neher, 1968:143-44.

/24/ Cf. David Hume: *Dialogues Concerning Natural Religion*, New York: Henry D. Aiken, 1948, part X.

/25/ Really? Despite the traditional character of the framework tale in the book, and the revealing indication of Ezek 14:14ff?

/26/ But what about Job 9:22 for example?

/27/ An expression which well illustrates the saying of Ricoeur's about the proverb's strategy of "*re-orientation by disorientation*" (1975:114).

/28/ It is from this perspective of Job-the-Servant of *YHWH* that one must consider the restoration of Job's fortunes. It parallels Isa 53:10b-12a.

WORKS CONSULTED

de Pury, R.
1955   *Job ou l'homme révolté.* Geneva: Labor et Fides.

Detweiler, R.
1978   *Story, Sign, and Self: Phenomenology and Structuralism as Literary Critical Methods.* Semeia Supplements. Philadelphia: Fortress and Missoula: Scholars Press.

Dhorme, E.
1926   *Le Livre de Job.* Paris: Gabalda.

Dornisch, L.
1975   "Symbolic Systems and the Interpretation of Scripture: An Introduction to the Work of Paul Ricoeur." *Semeia* 4:1–22.

Duesberg, H.
1939   *Les Scribes inspirés.* Paris: Desclée.

Eissfeldt, O.
1965   *The Old Testament. An Introduction.* Trans. P. R. Ackroyd. New York: Harper and Row.

Fox, M.
1980   "A Study of Job 38." *Semeia* 19:55–63.

Frankfort, H.
1948   *Kingship and the Gods.* Chicago: University of Chicago Press.

Frankfort, H., & H. A., et. al
1963   *Before Philosophy.* Baltimore: Penquin Books (repr.).

Friedlander, A. H. (ed.)
1976   *Out of the Whirlwind.* New York: Schocken Books.

Gammie, J. G.
1974   "Spatial and Ethical Dualism in Jewish Wisdom and Apocalyptic Literature." *JBL* 93:356–385.

Glatzer, N. N. (ed.)
1969   *The Dimensions of Job.* New York: Schocken Books.

Guillaume, A.
1968   *Studies in the Book of Job.* Leiden: Brill.

Habel, N. C.
1975 *The Book of Job*. Cambridge Bible Commentary. London, New York: Cambridge University Press.

Heidegger, M.
1968 *What is Called Thinking?* Trans. by J. G. Gray. New York: Harper and Row. [The French edition is *Qu'appelle-t-on Penser?* Paris: P.U.F., 1959]

Hengel, M.
1974 *Judaism and Hellenism*. Trans. by J. Bowden. London: SCM Press.

Heschel, A. J.
1971 *The Prophets*, Vol. II. New York: Harper Torchbooks.

Jacob, E.
1955 *Les Thèmes essentiels d'une Théologie de l'A. T.* Neuchâtel: Delachaux et Niestlé.

Jacobson, R.
1980 "Job and the Poetics of Authority: Some Deconstructions." *Semeia* 19:65–73.

Kallen, H. M.
1918 *The Book of Job as Greek Tragedy*. New York: Moffat, Yard, and Co. (repr. 1959).

Kaufmann, Y.
1960 *The Religion of Israel*. Trans. and abridged by M. Greenberg. Chicago: University of Chicago Press.

Kinnier Wilson, J. V.
1975 "A Return to the Problem of Behemoth and Leviathan." *VT* 25:1–14.

Kuntz, J. K.
1974 *The People of Ancient Israel*. New York: Harper and Row.

Kuyper, L. J.
1959 "The Repentance of Job." *VT* 9:91–94.

Lacocque, A.
1978 "A Return to a God of Nature?" *Sources of Vitality in American Church Life*. Ed. Robert L. Moore. Chicago: Exploration Press.

Larcher, C.
1950 *Le Livre de Job*. Paris: Cerf.

LeFèvre, A.
1949 "Le Livre de Job." *Dictionnaire de la Bible Supplément*. IV: 1073–1098.

Lods, A.
1950 *Histoire de la littérature hebraïque et juive*. Paris: Payot.

May, R.
1953 *Man's Search for Himself*. New York: Norton.

Neher, A.
1958 *Job* (unpublished lectures at Strasbourg University).
1968 "L'Echec dans la Perspective juive." *Les Hommes devant l'Echec*. Ed. J. Lacroix. Paris: P.U.F.

Pellauer, D.
1980 "Reading Ricoeur Reading Job." *Semeia* 19:73–84.

Pfeiffer, R.
1948² *Introduction to the Old Testament*. New York: Harper and Bros.

Pirot, L.
1913 *L'oeuvre exégétique de Théodore de Mopsueste, 350–428 ap. J.-C*. Rome: Scripta Pontificii Instituti Biblici.

Polzin, R. M.
1977 *Biblical Structuralism, Method and Subjectivity in the Study of Ancient Texts*. Semeia Supplements. Philadelphia: Fortress and Missoula: Scholars Press.

Pope, M. H.
1973³ *Job*. Anchor Bible. New York: Doubleday.

Resweber, J. P.
1971 *La Pensée de M. Heidegger*. Toulouse: Privat.

Ricoeur, P.
1960 *Finitude et Culpabilité II, La Symbolique du Mal*. Paris: Aubier.
1969 *Le Conflit des Interprétations, essais d'herméneutique*. Paris: Seuil
1975 "Biblical Hermeneutics." *Semeia* 4:29–148.
1976 *Interpretation Theory: Discourse and the Surplus of Meaning*. Fort Worth: Texas Christian University Press.

Robinson, H. W.
1939 *Suffering Human and Divine*. New York: Macmillan.
1955 *The Cross in the O.T.* Philadelphia: Westminster Press.

Sanders, P. S. (ed.)
1968 *Twentieth Century Interpretations of the Book of Job*. Englewood Cliffs: Prentice-Hall.

Scott, R. B. Y.
1971   *The Way of Wisdom in the Old Testament*. New York: Macmillan.

Sellin, E. and Fohrer, G.
1965   *Introduction to the Old Testament* Trans. by D. Green. Nashville: Abingdon.

Snaith, N.
1955   *The Distinctive Ideas of the Old Testament*. London: Epworth Press.

Steinmann, J.
1946   *Job*. Paris: Cerf.
1955   *Le Livre de Job*. Lectio Divina 16. Paris: Cerf.

Terrien, S.
1963   *Job*. CAT XIII. Neuchâtel: Delachaux et Niestlé.

Tsevat, M.
1966   "The Meaning of the Book of Job." *HUCA* 37:75ff.

Urbrock, W. J.
1976   "Oral Antecedents to Job: A Survey of Formulas and Formulaic Systems." *Semeia* 5:111–138.

van der Ploeg, J. P. M. and A. S. van de Wonde
1971   *Le Targoum de Job de la grotte de Qumran*. Leiden: Brill.

Vischer, W.
1933   "Hiob, ein Zeuge Jesu Christi." *Zwischen den Zeiten* 5. Munich: Kaiser.

von Rad, G.
1972a   *Wisdom in Israel*. Nashville, TN: Abingdon.
1972b   *Genesis*. Old Testament Library. Philadelphia: Westminster Press.

von Schelling, F. W. J.
1834   *Philosophische Untersuchungen über das Wesen der menschlichen Freiheit* . . . Reutingen: J. N. Ensslin (In English trans.: *Of Human Freedom*. Trans. by J. Gutmann. Chicago: The Open Court, 1936).

Zimmerli, W.
1978   *Old Testament Theology in Outline*. Trans. by D. E. Green. Atlanta: John Knox Press.

JOB 38 AND GOD'S RHETORIC

Michael V. Fox
University of Wisconsin-Madison

ABSTRACT

The primary task of exegesis is ascertaining the text's meaning, which is to be identified with the authorial intention. This understanding of "meaning" obliges the exegete to include questions of authorship (including literary-historical questions) in the investigation of the authorial intention. The brief study of Job 38 offered here focuses on one aspect of the text's form, its rhetoric, to see how this functions in conveying the message of persona and author.

My main concern in approaching a text is essentially the same as that of traditional literalist exegesis: to ascertain the meaning of the text, which is to say, the authorial intention. Following E. D. Hirsch, I would apply the term "meaning" only to the authorial meaning. All other understandings are better termed "significances." In Hirsch's words: "*Meaning* is that which is represented by a text; it is what the author meant by his use of a particular sign sequence; it is what the signs represent. *Significance*, on the other hand, names a relationship between that meaning and a person, or a conception, or a situation, or indeed anything imaginable" (8). The significance of a work includes both eisegesis and fruitful misunderstandings. These significances are in themselves worthy objects of study, and may be important in intellectual history, but they should not be confused with the *meaning* of the work.

The approach to interpretation that aims at the authorial intention assumes first of all that the authorial intention is accessible. This assumption cannot be proved, but it is one held in common by the author as he strives to make his words give expression to his thought or feeling and the reader as he works to recover that thought or feeling. Reading in this way is not psychologizing because it is concerned not with the author's mental processes and their causes but with the results of those processes. (It should be noted that "authorial intention" does not mean "authorial awareness"; it is possible to intend things one is not conscious of.) This approach rejects the assumption of semantic autonomy. Meaning is not inherent in a text, it is transmitted by a text. No one would bother to write if he did not assume that *his* meaning was conveyed by the text. If one writes a business letter or a scholarly article he is quite concerned that the reader grasp *his* intention, and if there is any area of uncertainty about its meaning he expects that he, the writer, will be taken as the final arbiter of its meaning. In most cases, of course, the author is not available for consultation, and in rare cases he may deliberately distort the meaning that he determined when he wrote the text, but the principle that the author determines the meaning stands. For most readers a text is a vehicle to an author's consciousness rather than a goal in itself, as is shown by the fact that a reader will commonly—and properly—ignore the text, even an autograph, in favor of the authorial intention, when encountering a manifest typographical error /1/.

The exegetical concern for authorial meaning naturally gives rise to two areas of inquiry: authorship and meaning.

Certain questions concerning authorship are important, sometimes essential, for understanding the meaning of the text. Biographical data such as the author's personal, social, historical, and intellectual background can be very useful in determining the author's meaning, and a rigid formalist exclusion of such data is unnecessary and can lead to distortions and misunderstandings. Data of this sort may be essential in the interpretation of texts closely linked to specific historical situations, such as political orations. The question concerning authorship that is often essential to understanding a text is the literary-historical question. When we read a text that is the result of a redactional process, we must attempt to be clear on what stage of development, i.e., what text, we are interpreting. There are two parts to this question. First is the problem of the "integrity" of the text: the authorship of a passage within a unit in relation to the authorship of the unit. The exegete must attempt to remove glosses, additions, and deliberate distortions by later authors. Such additions may be studied in their own right, as products of different authors with different concerns, but if not isolated they may change, distort, or trivialize the passage they appear in. Second, we ask about "originality": the authorship of the unit in relation to the authorship of the book. An ideal literary-historical study would result in a separation of layers and would outline the stages of production leading to the work in its final form. (For many texts there are several "final forms.")

As has been frequently stressed recently, each stage is a legitimate object of literary study, and the developmental dialectic itself is of interest. It is also legitimate to think of a collective authorship, if the final product is sufficiently unified to be treated as if it were the product of a single consciousness. The priestly document in the Pentateuch may be an example of this. Or a composite document may achieve unity through the work of a redactor. Then the redactor becomes the author whose intention we are inquiring about when we investigate the meaning of the work as a whole. But there has been a tendency in the literary study of the Bible to treat the final stage of textual development as sacrosanct, as the most significant if not the only authentic object of literary analysis. The so-called synchronic approach to a text, when it means exclusive concentration on the final form of a text, can become an easy way out that allows one simply to ignore the difficulties of literary history, and that can, in fact, detract from literary appreciation of a book. For later redactors can diminish the literary value of a work in attempting to improve it. Nahum Tate's redaction of King Lear has little *literary* interest, and we are unlikely to look upon it as the crowning achievement of a long process of authorship and redaction, though Tate saw himself as merely bringing polish and decorum to Shakespeare's work and making the allusive more explicit. The literary study of the Bible, whether performed under the labels of the New Criticism, Rhetorical Criticism, or Structuralism, has in practice tended to ignore the developmental, historical perspective. The historical perspective is the great achievement of the 19th century but is no more outmoded than the theory of evolution.

The major object of inquiry is the meaning or intention of the author; this inquiry is directed both at the unit in itself and the unit in relation to the work as a whole.

In approaching the meaning of the unit in itself, it is necessary first to define the scope of the unit—rhetorical criticism is useful here. The next step is philological analysis or *Einzelexegese*, and even though I will not be able to enter into this type of analysis here, I consider it the firmest foundation for any literary inquiry and the area of research most likely to produce truly innovative and lasting results. It is then necessary to look into formal or "literary" considerations, asking about the literary type or genre, style, rhetoric, imagery and topoi, allusions, and structure (by which I mean the plan or "surface structure").

But for many, perhaps most, types of discourse, ascertaining the paraphrasable content or propositional meaning—of the characters and of the author—is the concern most important to the author and most readers. Focus on the question of propositional meaning or paraphrasable content keeps other inquiries from producing mere cataloguing of formal data. It helps control the inquiry and keeps it anchored in the substance of the text. When this question is ignored the results are some of the most trivial examples of formalism, studies that meticulously amass data without contributing to our understanding of the work itself. Within the investigation of propositional meaning or statement, we may include the ideas of the unit, its didactic intent or message, the desired effect on the audience's attitudes and behavior, the plot line, and the portrayal of persons, groups and institutions, for these elements constitute the statement of the text and are at least partially paraphrasable. Finally, we may ask about the relation of the work to its literary tradition and to literature in general.

I would now like to ask some of these questions about Job 38:1–38. It is clear that the unit ends in 38:38; 38:39–40 belong to the second part of God's first speech. In the first part, God speaks about creation and the inanimate cosmos, in the second part about the relations between himself and the animal world and between the animal world and man.

First of all, the problem of authorship, the literary-historical question, has a direct bearing on exegesis. Our understanding of the context of God's speech is dependent on whether or not we regard the Elihu speeches (Job 32–37) as original, i.e., by the same author as the bulk of the book. Without the Elihu speeches we have a tremendously dramatic moment, where God suddenly and impressively appears and responds to Job's final summons (31:35–40). Neither Job nor the reader has a chance to catch his breath. If the Elihu speeches are original, they may be interpreted in a number of different ways. The author may be giving his own answer through Elihu. The importance of the theophany would then lie simply in God's appearing and implicitly confirming Elihu's words /2/. But why then does God not refer to Elihu in the epilogue to affirm the truth of his words? On the other hand, Elihu's speech might just be a rehash of the friends' words with just slightly different points of emphasis. In that case I cannot see why the author would bother putting him in. Or he may be offering a comic interlude. Elihu is indeed a comic character, with his two-chapter preamble in which he refers to the words that he himself is about to speak as a lot of gas about to bubble up from his stomach (32:19). But is this buffoonery a deliberate creation of the author of these chapters? This is an interesting possibility — one is reminded of Shakespeare's comic interludes before the dénouement. But in Elihu's case the humor does not continue throughout the speech, and there is nothing that signals humorous *intent* on the part of the author. The implicit author of these speeches does not set a distance between himself and his persona. When you consider further that Elihu does not appear in the epilogue with the other friends, though he should be chastised no less than they, it seems most likely that the Elihu speeches are a later addition, an addition that detracts from the dramatic force of the book.

The question of authorship arises also for individual passages in Job 38. Fohrer, for example, eliminates 38:19–20 as a "supplementing gloss" and 38:18 as a "varying gloss." But since it has not been established that the author avoids supplementing and varying his words—the contrary seems to be the case—there is no reason to eliminate these verses. From 38:13 and 15 Duhm eliminates phrases that imply the working of retribution: "Da werden abgeschüttelt von ihr die Frevler, Und stehen da wie zur Schande, Und es wird den Frevlern ihr Licht versagt, Und der erhobene Arm verschwindet" /3/. A decision on the originality of these phrases is essential. Is the author having God say that he does indeed punish the wicked so that God is affirming at least part of the doctrine of retribution? Such an affirmation is rather unexpected after Job has spoken so convincingly of God's injustice, but these words seem woven into their context, and furthermore 40:11–13, which are also woven into their context, likewise obliquely affirm God's punishment of the wicked. Furthermore, an orthodox gloss would probably be a straightforward statement, not a remark incidental to the description of another activity. 38:26–27 may indeed be secondary expansions (they are marked with an asterisk in the Hexapla). The motif of divine providence is out of place in this unit, while it would be in place in the unit beginning in 38:39. That unit speaks of God's marvelous wisdom and power in creation and maintenance of the natural order.

I will leave aside other problems of authorship, such as the date of composition and the intellectual background of the author, and turn to some of the matters subsumed under the question of meaning. I will concentrate on the meaning of the unit in itself, because the problem of the meaning is in this case the problem of the meaning of the book of Job and is too vast to be handled here.

I will consider some of the formal or "literary" characteristics of this unit and ask how they lead to an understanding of the unit's propositional content or message. In particular I will inquire into the rhetoric of this unit.

I am referring now to rhetoric in the classical sense, the art of influencing the audience. God certainly does influence Job; he brings him to a complete about-face that is sudden but not ironic or incongruous. I do not think it is God's appearance alone that influences Job, for then God's two speeches would be superfluous and would not provide an answer for anyone who does not get, and does not expect to get, a personal revelation. God's influence on Job—and the author's influence on *his* implicit audience—comes about through God's words. It is God's rhetoric that makes Job's about-face, his *tĕšuvah*, expected and natural.

God's main rhetorical technique in his first speech is the piling up of questions. The prominence given this rhetorical device indicates that it is not merely ornamental but a manner of communication instrumental in conveying the basic message of the speech. So it may be profitable to probe God's questions to see just what he is saying and why he is saying it in just this way.

The questions are clearly rhetorical questions, that is, they are questions that do not ask for information. There are two types of rhetorical questions. The first type is when the speaker asks a question and immediately answers it himself. This type of rhetorical question is merely an oratorical gesture, a device to capture and focus the audience's attention. The second type of rhetorical question is a statement in interrogative form. One asks a question so obvious that the answer is inevitable, either because the question is a tautology or—as is the case in Job 38—because it asks something which both the questioner and his auditor know, and which the questioner knows that his auditor knows, and which the auditor knows that the questioner knows he knows. The existence of this circle of knowing that one knows etc. is shown by the fact that the auditor realizes that he is not expected to answer the question. If one answers a rhetorical question a certain awkwardness ensues because the speaker senses a short-circuit in the communication. But a successful circuitry of knowledge sets up a special intimacy of communication. The auditor becomes aware first of a body of knowledge he shares with the speaker and then of the fact that they share knowledge. Such questions thus bind speaker and auditor closer together while making the auditor accept the speaker's claims out of his own consciousness rather than having the information imposed on him from the outside. This rhetorical effect occurs on two levels in the text before us. Both the ostensible auditor—Job—and the implicit auditor—the reader—answer the questions internally and experience the special awareness of the world called up by God's words.

God asks almost exclusively rhetorical questions in this unit. Most of the questions ask "who?", the inevitable but unspoken answer being "you, God": "Who set its measures?—for you know. Or who stretched a line over it?" (38:5). The parenthetical "for you know" is not sarcastic: God is reminding Job that he knows quite well who the architect and builder of the universe is. 38:7–11 describe in circumstantial clauses just how God proceeded in creation. The first-person in 38:9–10 shows that there is no question about who did this. Other questions ask what Job certainly knows: "Does the rain have a father?" (38:28), the understood answer being,—no, of course not; "or who begat the dewdrops"—no one, yet they exist. "Upon what are its (sc. the world's) sockets sunk?" The answer, as Job has already said in 26:7, is: *'al bĕlima*, "upon nothingness." Other questions require a humble "No, but you do" for an answer, e.g., "Have you ever commanded the morning, shown dawn its place?" (38:12). "Do you send bolts of lightning to go forth and say to you, 'Here we are'?" Only two of the questions are genuine questions: In 38:19 God asks, "What is the way to where the light dwells, and darkness—where is its place?" But here too the question is essentially a statement of Job's ignorance and is subordinated to a statement of his lack of power: " . . . so that you could take it to its territory, show (it) the path to its house" (38:20). The question in 38:24, "What is the way where the west wind divides, where the east wind spreads out on the earth?" is an actual question calling for information that Job cannot provide, but it too is closely bound with a "who" question (38:25) and is meant more to point to God's power than to stump Job.

If we rephrase the first part of God's speech in the indicative, the contrast in tone may make the rhetorical force of the question form more visible. 38:4-6 translated into the indicative come out: "You were nowhere when I founded the earth. (Admit this, if you indeed have understanding). *I* set its measures, as you know, and *I* stretched a line over it. Its sockets were sunk upon nothingness; *I* set its corner stone." Or, rephrasing 38:31-34: "*You* cannot bind the bonds of the Pleiades, nor can you release the bands of Orion. *You* cannot bring forth Mazzarot in its season, nor can you lead the Bear with her children. *You* do not know the laws of the heavens, nor can you bring about their rule on earth. *You* cannot raise your voice to the cloud, so that an abundance of water covers you" /4/. The tone, first of all, is entirely changed, and with it the portrayal of God's personality and his attitude to Job. God's remarks receive a harsh, bragging, bullying tone that they do not have in the original, mainly because in the indicative version God is not drawing Job in, not making him participate in the knowledge, but merely rubbing Job's face in his own feebleness. Through these rhetorical questions God does speak of his own wisdom and power and Job's relative weakness and ignorance, but he does so with compassion and gentleness, albeit a stern gentleness. God does remind Job of the limitations of his human wisdom, limitations Job knows quite well, but at the very same time he shows Job the significance of the wisdom Job does have. He has the ability to view the expanses of the universe and recognize God's orderly, constant rule. This is wisdom, and Job is criticized for not living up to the potentials of his wisdom. God demands humility, not humiliation.

God is not quizzing Job, not trying to squelch him by stumping him with hard questions. God overwhelms Job by showing him the obvious, by opening his eyes to what he already knows. If the theophany had been a revelation of something new or hidden, the book would not be so relevant for people who do not receive such a revelation. On the other hand, if God had merely tried to shut Job up by demonstrating Job's ignorance, he would be saying that there was no possible way for Job to see God's equity and orderly rule and thus would in effect be excusing him for speaking of God as arbitrary and immoral. Rather, God is saying to Job, You know very well that I and I alone created order and maintain it in the world, and I know that you know, and you know that I know that you know. This is the meaning of God's opening challenge: "Who is this that obscures providence ('eṣa) by ignorant words?" God implies that the 'eṣa, his plan for the world, is essentially manifest and known, and that Job is to be blamed for obscuring it, for obscuring a truth that he is really aware of.

We may also consider briefly the rhetorical force of the imagery. Through the tremendous scope of the imagery in time and space, God is making Job broaden his perspective, causing him to forget for the moment the pain of his own tragedy which distorted his view of God and the world and to look into the far reaches of time and space, to the time of creation when Job was not alive, to the expanses of space where Job cannot visit. The reader is carried along with Job on this imaginative journey and senses the immensity of God's rule. When the imagery suddenly shifts to the animal world in 38:39 and we hear minute details of God's care for his creatures, even raven chicks, the intimacy of God's concern for all his creatures becomes all the more impressive and evident.

All that God describes in chapters 38–41 are wonders, and in pointing to them God is pointing to the infinity of his own wisdom and to the limitation of Job's. But the limitation of Job's wisdom is not the main point. The main point is something that man can see quite clearly if he only broadens his perspective: God's wisdom and power in creating and ruling the cosmos. And this rule includes justice in the human sphere, as 38:13 and 15, then 40:11–13, imply.

NOTES

/1/ Ricoeur presents a less extreme position on semantic autonomy than the one I criticize here. He rejects the "fallacy of the absolute text" (30). But it is not clear to me how he reconciles his rejection of that fallacy with his acceptance of semantic autonomy. If inscription does indeed entail "disconnection of the mental intention of the author from the verbal meaning of the text, of what the author meant and what the text means" (29–30), then does not authorial meaning become merely a historical datum which has no greater relevance to the text's meaning than does the interpretation of each and every reader?

/2/ Thus, essentially, Y. Kaufmann (334–338).

/3/ Reading tšbt for tšbr (183).

/4/ The emphasis on the subject ("I," "you") corresponds to the emphasis implicit in the form of the questions, since they ask *who* did such and such, not *what* was done.

WORKS CONSULTED

Black, Edwin
    1978   *Rhetorical Criticism*. Madison: University of Wisconsin Press.

Duhm, Bernhard
    1897   *Das Buch Hiob*. Leipzig: J. C. B. Mohr.

Fohrer, Georg
    1963   *Das Buch Hiob*. KAT XVI. Gütersloh: Gerd Mohn.

Hirsch, E. D.
    1967   *Validity in Interpretation*. New Haven: Yale University Press.

Kaufmann, Yehezkel
    1960   *The Religion of Israel*. Chicago: University of Chicago Press.

Ricoeur, Paul
    1976   *Interpretation Theory: Discourse and the Surplus of Meaning*. Fort Worth: Texas Christian University Press.

SATANIC SEMIOTICS, JOBIAN JURISPRUDENCE

Richard Jacobson
University of Wisconsin-Madison

ABSTRACT

The essay approaches the book of Job as a construction whose meaning is to be sought in its formal aspect: relentless contradiction. The juridical figure which recurs in the book serves as emblem and evidence of the centrality of a dialectical process. In the final analysis, the book represents a competition for an hermeneutic privilege, won (in a sense) by those who *represent* the argument by authorizing the book.

1. Form and Meaning

In the book of Job, its form, the representation on the synchronic plane of an historical process, *is* its meaning. The "book," in this sense, means the final form of the book, itself the evidence and substance of an historical dialectic. The relentlessness of the dialectic, and its insufficiency to deal with the external reality it purports to discuss, is of the essence. Ultimately the book succeeds in becoming a sign of itself; not only does it contain repeated contradiction, it signifies relentless alternation, a primary uncertainty, an essential paradox.

Ricoeur, of course, pointed up the historical process in the evolution of Biblical books as grounds for discounting the validity of a structural analysis (1974). In the final redaction one finds an "intellectual working-out" in which quite conscious statements are revised and re-worked across the generations. While the characterization of the development of the Old Testament as an intellectual re-thinking strikes me as apt, the conclusion that a variety of methods developed by the structuralist (and post-structuralist) schools are thereby inapplicable is less valid. Given that one may mean a good many things one does not consciously intend, both because of the process of overdetermination of mental constructs, and because of the (related) nature of signification itself (one sign necessarily implying some other sign as its interpretant, repeated *ad infinitum*), even a canonical structural analysis may uncover patterns and relations—a "structure of determinate differences"—of which one or all of the producers of the *travail intellectuel* may not have been aware. Or even if they were aware of the logical relations, the very presence of these structures may point to a range of significant data leading to other, extra-textual, correlations.

In any event, the development of semiotic thinking since the early sixties, including in particular the post-structuralist trend (such as the work of the *Tel Quel* group) or even apparently anti-structuralist positions (Foucault), not to speak of the continued development of Lévi-Strauss's own methods, suggests that the dispositions of recent semiotic analysis may be highly instructive for the reading of the Old Testament—along with all other cultural texts.

2. Enoncé/Enonciation: Histoire/Discours

The French linguist Emile Benveniste, beginning with a discussion of pronouns in the Indo-European languages, noted the presence in all utterance of two levels or planes of speech, which he termed *histoire* (story) and *discours* (discourse). In any utterance, one can isolate what is told from those signs which indicate in some way the personal participation of a teller and a hearer. Applying this insight to narrative, Roland Barthes identified in stories the equivalent (or nearly equivalent) dichotomy of narration (*énonciation*) and narrative (*énoncé*), both located *within* the text. Thus one can find in any text evidence of a *textual* narrator and a textual "audience," again distinguished by the axis of personality/impersonality. While Barthes' explanation of this fact of the text has been subjected to some searching scrutiny (Culler: 199–201), it does reflect a real and universal characteristic, which is none other than the inscription in the text of the lost moment in history when texts were told, social, communicative products. The presence in the text of the signs of narration is a fossil of an earlier stage in the history of telling, when speaking itself was, more so than now, an event. In sum the inscription in the text of a representation of the situation of speaking is the recapitulation of the reality for which it is a substitute.

Just as the narrative is embedded within the moment of narration (not necessarily in a chronological, but in an a-chronic sense), so in larger units the book of Job consists of multiple embedded discourse, approximately as represented below.

"Real" Frame: Authors ———— book ———— Audience
                   (Redactors)

Prose Frame: God ———— wager ———— the Satan

Poetic Discourse: Comforters ———— debate ———— Job

What makes this book unusual, though hardly unique, is that actions and words or perhaps more specifically, internal and external dispositions, are equated. In both story and discourse (i.e., the account of the discussion and the prose framework) the narrative seeks to *achieve conviction*. God seeks to convince the Satan, the "comforters" seek to convince Job, and apparently the redactors seek to convince the potential audience. The result striven for is a change of mind. It is very like a courtroom, an analogy suggested not only by the occurrence in both places of a conflict of interpretations, but also because Job quite explicitly and frequently introduces the metaphor of a courtroom, typically by indicating its *inapposition* to his situation—the courtroom is a *failed metaphor*, inscribed only to be undercut, no less than each statement made in the course of the debate is a failed proposition concerning the world. We are repeatedly presented with inadequate arguments until the book comes itself to represent the inadequacy of argument.

Legal and juridical discourse pervade the book, to an extent not fully reflected in the standard translations. The Satanic figure and his jurisprudence comprise one outstanding example. When God holds his royal court, for example, he finds among his other courtiers a particular official, the Satan, whose function (possibly derived from the "eyes and ears of the Persian King" as represented by Herodotus, or from the universal need of monarchs for derogatory information) is to "go to and fro (*šut*) in the world" and presumably to report on what he has seen (Tur-Sinai: 38–45). When the Lord points out Job's outstanding character, Satan offers a cynical and rather coarse version of reward-theodicy when he suggests that Job's sterling qualities are not "for nought" (*ḥinnam*). It would be quite another story if Job were not so well off. God in his two confrontations with this officer invites attention to Job's loyalty or persistence—a loyalty substantiated by Job's resignation (1:21; 2:10). The Job of the prose frame, and the rather empirical divine potentate, both seem to deny the simplicity of the reward-theodicy.

Most to the point in terms of a bolder discussion of justice, set in a legal framework, is the speech of the rather different, poetic, Job in Job 9. Some of the technical legal vocabulary must be restored to the translation, as follows:

> But how can man be acquitted against God? (9:2)
> Should he argue against him, he cannot answer one of a thousand (arguments).
> How much less could I answer him, and choose out my words against him,
> Whom, though I were innocent, yet I would not answer, nor appeal to the mercy of the court . . . (9:14–15)
> (sc. Perhaps) it is all one: He destroys the perfect and the wicked . . .
> The land is given to the hand of the wicked; he covereth the faces of its judges:
> If it is not so, who then (will refute me)? (9:22, 24; Tur-Sinai, *ad loc.*)

After pointing out the disproportion between the adversaries in an imagined courtroom, and the paradox of one individual serving as both prosecutor and judge ("Though I were innocent, my mouth would condemn me," 9:20), Job presents one bold hypothesis: God either does not care for justice at all, or deliberately fosters injustice. Both of these propositions at least allow for the resolution of the contradiction—powerful god fosters justice BUT allows an innocent Job to suffer. The resolution favored by the comforters—Job is not innocent—is not true. Job is forced to conjecture two other resolutions: God is unjust, or God is not powerful—he has turned over his power to others who are corrupt.

The precise history of the text of Job, of course, is lost, and numerous hypotheses have been advanced to account for the book's development and numerous internal contradictions. Whatever the history may have been, something rather like the account in Jastrow (64–81) would adequately account for the text we have. The earliest stage of the story would be the original folktale, revised by the first poet who inserted Job's lament (Job 3) and one or all of the cycles of dialogue. The nature poem in Job 28 was at one point the close of the poem. The speech of Job ending with the tag "the words of Job are ended" (31:40) may have come before Job 28. The speeches of Elihu were later appended, and finally the speech of Yahweh from the whirlwind, itself interpolated with the mythical monster fragments, was inserted just before the resumption and close of the prose frame story.

Not only the development of the book in these broad outlines, but the final stages of virtually all of Job's speeches, represent an elaborate diachronic dialectic. Obviously, the dialogue between Job and the comforters involves contradiction. Similarly, Elihu must claim to contradict both Job *and* the comforters ("They had found no answer, and yet had condemned Job," 32:3). But the contradiction is a specious one, and may have been intended to fail: despite Elihu's tone of authority, he adds no new matter. It might be argued that after the first cycle of dialogue, nothing the comforters say advances the argument: they represent merely the continuation without change or development of the positions staked out earlier. The book could go on forever representing the failure of resolution, the incapacity of the argument to advance, had not a late redactor inserted Yahweh's speech from the whirlwind, which comments upon the whole earlier discourse and supersedes it by negation.

But contradiction — because of the diachronic editorial process — is rife even in the smaller units of text. Just as it is theoretically possible to explain the disorder of such a prophetic collection as Isaiah by seeing how pious editors must have interpolated auspicious prophecies to counter prophecies of doom, so in many of Job's speeches utterly incongruous pious remarks are inserted. One example will suffice for many: following Job's elaborate restatement of the central problem, beginning "Wherefore do the wicked live, grow old, and are mighty in power," (21:7) comes an assertion that the wicked do indeed suffer grievously (e.g., 27:13–23).

A perfect epitome of the diachronic dialectic occurs in one of the most often quoted passages in Job. Consider 13:15 as it appears in the Masoretic Text:

hen yiqṭ^{e}leniy lo' (K^{e}tib—Q^{e}re: lo) 'ayaḥel 'ak-d^{e}rakay 'el-pana(y)w 'okiyaḥ

This verse is translated in the Authorized Version: "Though he slay me yet will I trust in Him, but I will maintain mine own ways before Him." The AV translators followed the Q^{e}re annotation, which replaces the *aleph* in *lo'* with a *waw*—that is the negation in the consonantal text is replaced by a pronoun. Even assuming the accuracy of '*ayaḥel* as "trust," the consonantal text reads "I shall *not* trust." A pious annotator clearly found an easy way out, replacing "not" with "in him." In fact, there are several possibilities of meaning: *'ayaḥel* might mean, depending on vocalization, "be disappointed," "wait," "be put at rest." Tur-Sinai translates, conserving the Q^{e}re, "If he slay me — I am waiting for it, but I will reprove his ways to his face." ("his" instead of "my" ways depends only on exchanging the *yodh* for a *waw*, and accords with the usual meaning of YKḤ in Job, "reprove"). The annotator thus engages in a dialogue with the text before him, placing one letter "in erasure"—present but absent. To his eye the contradiction across time must have appeared as a needed correction, but little could he know that to a later reader it is the *mutual* contradiction which stands out, not the pious correction.

But there is more to contradiction than this. Contradiction in the broad sense, including paradox, willed and unwilled, and dissonance, creates a kind of alienation of meaning; it spatializes signification and makes it remote. Faced with contradiction or dissonance, the mind oscillates in search of a certain meaning which is always somewhere *else*: seek it and it is lost. But the mind still seeks.

3. Deconstruction and Authority

It is time to invoke another post-structuralist point of departure: the idea of deconstruction. To the deconstructive critic, texts are assumed to offer fictions as truths, and then, inadvertently—or by an intended appearance of inadvertance—to disclose their inauthenticity (Robertson). As noted above, the traces of the historicity of the textual process can be found in the text: presented to our eyes as a synchronous whole, it "deconstructs" promptly into a series of failed confrontations with the teachings of much of the rest of the Old Testament, or of institutionalized religion generally. It did not require a Deuteronomy to introduce the idea of reward and punishment, though no doubt that book did much to formalize the doctrine in the history of the Israelites. After the failure of all attempts to resolve the conflict between belief and exprience, Yahweh, the specifically Israelite divinity, must be imported to speak the all but final words, as Professor Lacocque reminds us above.

I have argued elsewhere that Authority is typically represented as a form of Absence (1978), certainly in the Israelite tradition and in large measure elsewhere. But absence may be said, paradoxically, to extend itself in more that one dimension. It is straightforwardly represented in the empty Sepulchre, or the space above the cherubim. But it is present no less in the spatialized conception of the *alibi*. Authority *is* alibi: it is not *here*; it is in the other place, until I seek it there, when I find it is yet elsewhere. And so the source of meaning, the locus of certainty, oscillates, never to find a specific place. But those who claim it as adherents, those who seek to exercise it, must find some means of *representing* it. The exercise of authority—at least in texts and likely in life—turns out to be the manipulation of absence, an absence which may be spatial, conceptual, or both.

Consider the central *aporia* (and note that the term itself is a spatialization of an intellectual incapacity) of the text, an *aporia* which emerges from Job's conceptual paradox: God cannot be both all-powerful and just. Just action implies limitation: power cannot be both unlimited and also just. (Of course, power may be limited by the one who wields it. A gesture in this direction is made by the divine potentate when he restricts the Satan's power over Job's life.) But if the wielder of power consistently chose not to exercise a certain power, we would not know that he had the power. In texts, and likely in the text of reality as well, power must be used or it does not exist. But justice, as Socrates teaches Euthyphro, is an independent and *a priori* consideration by which gods no less than people may be judged. Justice must be conceptually separated from divinity to allow for a just world. Merge justice and divinity, and Yahweh is no better than Thrasymachus. Consider the latter's classic statement of the "non-law" or "non-justice" position: "In all states alike 'right' has the same meaning, namely what is for the interest of the party established in power, and that is the strongest. So the sound conclusion is that what is 'right' is the same everywhere: the interest of the stronger party" (Bornford: 338). It would appear that the jurisprudence of the book of Job is ultimately Thrasymachian: justice does not stand apart from divinity, but as Yahweh implies from the whirlwind, both power and right are one, and the Accuser indeed the agent of the Judge.

God of course wins his wager: Job is indeed righteous despite being punished "gratuitously" (*l^eḥinnam*). Job's relative victory over his interlocutors, however, is incomplete. The text tells us he is made whole, with damages (depending upon the meaning of *šib'anah*), but his victory deconstructs as soon as the reader recognizes the incommensurability of persons and property, or of individuals and categories. Children may be replaced by other children, but the child lost can never be replaced. In any case, Job may be proven righteous, but God cannot be proven just. Authority is never just—and rarely *present*. It only *has effect*, and may be *recognized*.

Within the story or narrative (*histoire*, *énoncé*) signs of discourse abound. God takes on the voice of the debater not only in his rhetorical questions (38:2,4,5,etc.) but also in the signs of discourse with Job: *hineh-na' behemot 'ašer 'asitiy 'imak*— "take note, if you please, of Behemoth which I made with thee" (40:15). The particle *na'* not only represents real speech, but the divine invitation is an index of domination as well. The particle unites the narration and the narrative, turning the two inside out as the various addressees of all the levels of discourse are created subjects of the divine "I made." We are rendered, through a textual and linguistic process, congruent subjects of power.

4. Hermeneutics and Power

In a certain sense the competition between Job and his comforters is about the *right to interpret*. It has been noted more than once that the power to interpret is real power in a society. The comforter and Job struggle for authority to read the signs of the past and the present. Like the self-proclaimed protectors of an imagined *status quo* in any other time or place, they claim to be the privileged heirs of the collective past: "Remember, please, who ever perished being innocent, or where were the righteous cut off?" asks Eliphaz (4:7). By seeking control over the hermeneutic privilege, by arrogating the collective experience to themselves, the comforters assert their further authority over the concepts governed by the interplay of signs in the text. It might be said that the closing portions of the book are a triumphant account of a logical failure. We know how in society logical failures, or those who recognize them, are typically dealt with: by the application of sufficient force to produce silence. And we know sadly that something rather like belief generally follows such an application: *credo quia absurdum.*

Faced with logical paradox and the claim still maintained by Job against the invocation of traditional authority, the author must introduce God to assert a measure of interpretive authority: man at least cannot understand. It is God who retains the privilege of a certain inflection, the sign of the question. Job, it is true, asks numerous questions, but only God asks the questions which have no answer. This authority, governed by the final author as the definitive statement in a dialectic across time and space, is neither here nor there, nor does he even address directly the question of justice. He dodges the question by asserting the disproportion between what humans can know and what there is to know. The whirlwind is without question an "alibi."

The authority then is presented to us by an invocation, a gesture, an inflection, a re-presentation. At its most effective, Authority, in the text of reality as in literature or law, is a *citation*. It is a gesture toward an absent past presented as the possession of the speaker. Bildad to be sure offers empty precedents (e.g., 8:8–10), but the authors bring in God to speak. Let us not forget though that *God does not speak*: a text speaks in his place. Thus in the final analysis, the one with the broadest horizons, the ultimate authority exercised is practiced by the authors of the book in the form of a displacement. And in so exercising their power, they signal to us the means by which we may make ourselves free.

WORKS CONSULTED

Barthes, Roland
1966 "Introduction à l'analyse structurale des récits." *Communication* 8:1-27.

Benveniste, Emile
1971 *Problems in General Linguistics.* Trans. M. E. Meek. Coral Gables, FL: University of Miami Press.

Cornford, F. M., tr.
1945 *The Republic of Plato.* New York and London: Oxford University Press.

Culler, Jonathan
1975 *Structuralist Poetics.* Ithaca, NY: Cornell University Press.

Jacobson, Richard
1977 "Law, Ritual, Absence." *Hartford Studies in Literature* 9: 164-174.
1978 "Absence, Authority, and the Text." *Glyph* 3: 137-47.

Jastrow, Morris
1920 *The Book of Job: Its Origin, Growth, and Interpretation.* Philadelphia: Lippincott.

Ricoeur, Paul
1974 "Structure and Hermeneutics." Pp. 27-61 in his *The Conflict of Interpretations.* Evanston, IL: Northwestern University Press [from 1963].

Robertson, Mary
1979 "Does the River Liffey Freeze Well? A Critique of Margot Norris' *The Decentered Universe of Finnegans Wake.*" *Semiotic Scene* 2: 169-79.

Tur-Sinai, N. H.
1967 *The Book of Job: A New Commentary.* Jerusalem: Kiryath Sepher.

READING RICOEUR READING JOB

David Pellauer
Vanderbilt University

ABSTRACT

Because my position in this discussion is that of someone who is familiar with Ricoeur's hermeneutical theory but who is not a specialist in exegesis, this essay undertakes an "experimental" reading of Job 38 based on my understanding of that theory, hoping in this way to further our grasp of the possibilities and limits of this theory. I begin with a review of Ricoeur's work which touches on the following points: the need for interpretation, the possibility of interpretation, the three characteristics of the text that ground interpretation, the role of sense and reference in the meaning of a text, and the relation of interpretation to subjectivity. In passing I also note a question regarding the role and status of concepts in such a theory.

On this basis, I then consider Job 38 as clearly a problem for interpretation, as a problem for me as a theologian in light of the fact that Job claims "to see" God, and in terms of Ricoeur's three characteristics of the text. My conclusions are that the fact that Job does more than simply acknowledge Yahweh as the one who questions him points to a fundamental theological paradox inherent in theophanies inasmuch as the appearance of something other than God can at the same time be an appearance of God, and that more is at issue in the meaning of this text than just some doctrine of providence.

To conclude, in light of this interpretation, and of Ricoeur's theory, I raise two questions for a general theory of hermeneutics. (1) Can such a theory, contrary to Ricoeur's hermeneutical wager, allow for the possibility that a text might not make sense? And if so, under what conditions? (2) How do we allow for the possibility of historical-critical inquiry for its own sake as a legitimate enterprise, yet demonstrate that the conditions of intelligibility that make its assertion possible and meaningful have their basis in a wider theory that acknowledges the concrete, particular subjectivity of the investigator?

My position in this discussion is that of someone who knows something about recent hermeneutical theory, but who is an amateur when it comes to the historical study and exegesis of biblical texts. I do not possess the requisite languages nor have I served the necessary apprenticeship required by this discipline. I have chosen, therefore, to approach our specimen text experimentally in terms of my understanding of Paul Ricoeur's hermeneutical theory, hoping in this way to illustrate how I think this theory might carry over into interpretation praxis. The advantage of such an undertaking is that in return it may make possible a clearer understanding of this theory. To this end, I shall begin by offering several comments on Ricoeur's theory in terms of its presentation of the hermeneutical task. Then turning to our text, Job 38, I shall attempt to show one way this theory may be applied to it. Finally, in light of this reading, I shall venture two comments concerning further elaboration of Ricoeur's theoretical insights.

The need for interpretation, Ricoeur holds, arises from our need to respond to the distanciation inherent in our relation to the semantic autonomy of texts. Texts are to be understood broadly as including any inscription of human discourse (or action), including monuments and works of art as well as documents, though for our purposes, we may limit our discussion to written examples such as the book of Job.

Distanciation is a problem because, while it is a necessary component of the dialectic of participation and distanciation that characterizes and constitutes our existence, it threatens to be alienating. A text may be so foreign to us as to be beyond comprehension, hence as having nothing to say. The hermeneutic wager is that this is not the case, so that interpretation seeks to discover and appropriate the meaning proffered to us. This meaning depends, as does distanciation itself, upon the fact that, as inscribed, every text outlasts and therefore escapes its original setting, including its author's intention and its original audience. It is this semantic autonomy of the text that implies that its meaning is potentially available to anyone who knows how to read and interpret it properly—hence the need for a theory of interpretation and its application.

This formulation of the hermeneutical task is itself based on a prior understanding of the nature of language as discourse that makes possible the transition from speaking to writing and back again. More precisely, discourse can occur as either spoken or written, for it is the use of the elements of language (vocabulary and syntax) by somebody to say something about something to somebody (even oneself). The assumption that discourse is always about something—that even when mistaken, we intend to say something about something (cf. Ricoeur, 1976:36)—is the basis of what I have called the hermeneutical wager. If an act of discourse or a text is always about something, and if this statement about something endures, there is always something to be interpreted and applied to any subsequent situation or context.

What endures is the meaning of what is said, what passes away is the event of saying it, the utterance or writing of this phrase at this moment. This meaning combines both a sense, or propositional content, and a reference, where the referential aspect points back to the originator (more as the implied than as the actual author) and forward to a world that the audience might inhabit. It is what is "understood" in any "instance of discourse," or any reenactment or restatement of that discourse. Similarly, what endures through the semantic autonomy of a text, and what any reader understands, is the meaning of this text, including again both sense and reference.

It follows that the process of interpretation has to do with the discovery of this meaning, or some portion of it, and its appropriation. This process moves from the text as inscribed to a new (or renewed) event of discourse that speaks to us (or to our imagination). It is guided by those characteristics of a text that make possible the inscription of discourse.

To date, Ricoeur has identified three such characteristics, all of which need to be understood as producing the text rather than simply as categorizing its results: it is organized as a work, exemplifying some genre, on the basis of a unique individual style. Given these typical features of any text, we have not only some means of construing its parts and whole (in an initial act of understanding best characterized as a guess), but also certain structures that may be explored as generating and bearing the text's meaning. In a stronger statement of this latter point, we may say that such structures "explain" why a text has the meaning it does have.

In fact, I think more precision is required here in regard to two points. First, as referring to the internal, constant features of a text, style, genre, and over-all organization are more indicative of sense than of reference. Since reference points beyond the text, it can only be determined by taking the reader and his or her situation into account. Thus it would seem to follow, although Ricoeur himself has not drawn this conclusion, that literary criticism or biblical exegesis might be able to state the sense of any given text, at least given the context of some specifiable method such as form-criticism or rhetorical analysis. This sense would vary only as a function of changes in our conceptual knowledge and understanding, or as a result of better insight into the nature of the *Urtext* and/or its historical setting, although these would never be sufficient to convey the text's meaning *for us*.

I am suggesting such a conclusion for the sake of discussion because, if correct, it may provide some basis for properly assessing the role and value of such current approaches to texts as form-criticism or redaction-criticism within a general theory of interpretation that would include both literary criticism and biblical exegesis. On Ricoeur's terms, such knowledge concerning the sense of a text—and it is knowledge in the sense of being the confirmable result of a canon of stateable procedures—is not the meaning hermeneutics seeks. It is at best the basis for a new inquiry, one whose procedures are less easily stated or codified because the "subjective" aspect of this undertaking finds insufficient resources for its explication in our current epistemological and ontological theories. We are still too vague, in other words, when it comes to the nature of subjectivity, not to speak of having inadequate insight into its operations. To illustrate this, it will suffice to recall that the subject is usually formally conceived of as a pure knower, the ego in the *ego cogito cogitatum* model characteristic of modern thought. This ego lacks the personal identity as well as the contingent particularity of concrete existence that are precisely the necessary conditions for any appropriable meaning and any appropriation of this meaning on Ricoeur's terms.

This point is important because Ricoeur's suggestion has often been that the way to the existing, actual subject, not just to a new self-understanding, is precisely through the process of interpretation and its outcome. For example: "It is the text, with its universal power of world disclosure, which gives a self to the ego" (1976:95). As I hope we shall see as we proceed, it is this new version of the hermeneutical circle—I must understand texts in order to be a self as well as to understand myself and my world—that makes Job 38, and the book of Job generally, such a fascinating choice for any attempt to examine Ricoeur's hermeneutic by way of a specific text to be interpreted.

Second, and I shall only briefly raise this point as a possible topic for subsequent investigation and discussion, Ricoeur's use of the sense-reference distinction in *Interpretation Theory* leaves unclear the role and status of concepts in his theory and its application. Yet in his more recent *The Rule of Metaphor*, he says that "Interpretation is the work of concepts" (1977:302). What is more, this question seems all the more important in light of the emphasis in this volume on the possibility of conceptual language and knowledge as opposed to poetic language (and "knowledge"). I raise the question here because for *Interpretation Theory* the sense of a text is linked at least in part to the propositional content of its sentences, though it is more than their simple sum. Such propositional content is a function of predication not just of words, hence it is not a concept. The question, therefore, is where and how concepts arise. Then, how do they function? (They are clearly used in propositions.) Are they somehow to be located in the referential component of meaning, or do they depend on the sense-reference interaction in the act of interpretation? Or, as *The Rule of Metaphor* suggests (1977:295–303), can they be shown to be constituted through the interaction of different spheres of discourse? In any case, this problem needs to be pursued further if we are to formulate adequately Ricoeur's hermeneutical theory in its wider implications and the rules for its use.

But our more immediate concern is for Job 38, so let us now turn to that text. Clearly Job is a text that has endured close to the heart of our tradition. Yet in many ways it seems as distanciated or potentially alienated from us as any text can be. A look at the scholarship concerning it accentuates this fact, as a short search in the library demonstrates.

On the one hand, we know the history of interpretations of Job well enough to recognize how much earlier Christian and Jewish commentators let their presuppositions too quickly domesticate the problem of Job's suffering. Recent secular, literary critical approaches have taken this issue more seriously, but it is not clear that they have been any more successful in explaining or understanding Job, too often having been content to reduce him to a type of existential anguish and rebellion, or at least their precursor, when they are not caught up in the question of genre. Is Job a comedy or a tragedy? Or somehow both? As an attempt to get Job into familiar, thus more manipulatable categories, such debates signify in their own way the problem of distanciation.

On the other hand, if we look at the highly refined and technical literature put forth by contemporary biblical scholars, it is apparent that Job remains one of the more difficult topics confronting them. Indeed, it seems a fair generalization to say that the study of Job remains largely a question of textual criticism and philosophy rather than that of interpretation in Ricoeur's sense of this term. Because no book of the Old Testament contains so many difficult or even unknown terms, much of the interesting scholarship turns upon questions of emendation or comparative linguistics, the controversies in this area being still so lively that attempts to speak of the "meaning" of Job obviously bear a tentative or speculative *caveat*. Or at least they must be read that way.

Still, even though we have to assume some version of Job 38 as our starting point (Pope), where the necessity of such an assumption may be taken as partial confirmation of Ricoeur's point about the problem of distanciation and its implications, we may risk applying his further suggestions regarding the importance of the characteristics of inscribed discourse to see what happens, all the time acknowledging as best we can our own subjectivity. This last factor is important because the editorial comment in 38:1 works against any attempt to confine our reading to just chapter 38. That this passage is said to be Yahweh's *answer* to Job implies either a prior question, however difficult it may be to specify, or the need for such a reply, however difficult it may be to specify. It also points to the larger context of at least the verse passages in Job, including what follows this particular portion of that text. I emphasize this because the question of the meaning of this passage for me insofar as I am a theologian is tied up with questions arising out of what Job says in response to Yahweh's questions; I refer especially to 42:5b where he indicates that his repentance turns on the fact that he has "seen" God in the phenomena mentioned in chapters 38–41. How, to put it briefly, are we either to explain or to understand the theophany recounted in chapter 38 as a theophany that involves or culminates in a vision of God?

This question is reinforced by my surprise at how commentators have rapidly passed over this question, if they raise it at all. Typically, they move quickly to a contrast between hearing about God and seeing God as though this were sufficient to explicate this passage. The following three examples may serve to illustrate what I mean. (See also, Pope:289; Lévêque:525–26; Dhorme:646; Rowley:342.)

> Vision is here contrasted as direct personal experience of what a person is and does with hearing as knowledge at second-hand, knowledge of some other's experience or report of that person, knowledge, which, even if not mingled with error, as was the traditional doctrine of God, what had been passed on to Job, must at best be blurred and indistinct; for the contrast, cp. 28:21f., Ps. 48:9 (the stories of the fathers about God [cp. Ps. 44:2] verified by the direct sight, i.e., experience, of the present generation). The vision spoken of is not the sight of any form or appearance of God; for there is no indication that Job is conceived as having seen such, and, moreover, the sight of an appearance or outward form is just as far as hearing from giving direct, intimate, true knowledge (cp. Is 11:3, Is. 16:7). What Job has seen, i.e., experienced, is just what he had wished to see (19:37) viz. that God is not against him or estranged from him; and his wish has been more than fulfilled, for the vision [sic!] has come to him before death (Driver and Grey:372–3).

> There is no question of a vision of God. Job simply uses the figure to emphasize the deeper conviction he now possesses of the divine power. It is *as if* he had actually seen the great works of God, instead of hearing of them by the tradition of the fathers (Kissane:292, my emphasis).

> The allusion to visual perception should not lead us to believe that there was indeed a theophany in the full sense of the word or that the Lord's appearance imprinted its shape of dazzling light upon the patient's retina. Hebrew usage as well as the immediately preceding context (vs. 5a) shows precisely what the poet had in mind: an antithesis between the traditional belief by hearsay, inherited through the intellect from a past now dead, and the actual experience, as piercing as burning coals, as real as death, as warm as life. Job left the mediacy of belief for the immediacy of faith (Terrien:239).

Ricoeur himself, who strongly emphasizes the problem of suffering and how to endure suffering in his references to Job, does not address this problem either (see 1974:351, 461–2; 1965:303). Yet applying Ricoeur's hermeneutical theory to this text, and through it to Job 38, I suggest, depends on answering the question I have raised. At least this will be my own presupposition with regard to this text.

Actually applying or attempting to apply Ricoeur's suggested criteria reinforces this question. The genre of chapter 38 purports to be a dialogue, thus pointing however indirectly to a sender and a receiver, to use Greimas's categories. Yet only Yahweh speaks, doing so more as a prosecuting attorney than as a partner in some I-Thou model of conversation. Note that we are told that he speaks and what he says, not that he appears.

That the adversary nature of the question-answer format demanded by Yahweh's challenge in 38:2-3 is more Socratic than Platonic in tone may be one reason so many critics characterize the style of this chapter as ironic (e.g., Dhorme:lix; Rowley:309; von Rad, 1972:223). This label conveys essentially all that I have been able to discover concerning the style at work here, if we take style in Ricoeur's individuating sense and exclude comparisons of Job as a whole with its Egyptian and Babylonian parallels, comparisons that to my knowledge do not extend so far as a detailed analysis of chapter 38. (Von Rad, 1965, is not sufficient.) So perhaps more could be done with regard to the question of generative style on the basis of a fuller explication of the concept of irony being applied. For example, we might ask why we should not say that Yahweh's questions, or at least some of them, are not better characterized as sardonic or even sarcastic in tone and intention. As Terrien says, "Let us admit that the irony of God is bewildering. It is not even an especially delicate species of sarcasm" (226). Would further development of such distinctions add anything to our grasp of Job's style?

I can only raise these questions here. I am not sure as to how to pursue them further on Ricoeur's terms. However, having said something about genre and style, what about structure? What I find striking here given my theological interests is the way "who?" questions alternate with questions about Job's knowledge or ability. My more linguistically learned colleagues in this enterprise may be able to confirm this in greater detail, but it seems to me that the verbs translated as signifying "knowing" and "doing" in this passage are so closely linked as to require that knowing something entails being able to do or perform it and vice-versa.

If this supposition is correct, the "can you?" and the "do you know?" questions that structure this chapter may be taken as equivalent, thereby emphasizing the more significant alternation with inquiries as to who created the earth and is capable of affecting it at will. If so, the following "structure" may be discerned in Job 38.

    I.   Introductory passage stating the call for a response
         1. editorial comment, v. 1
         2. Yahweh's challenge, vv. 2-3

II. First series of alternating questions
   1. who created the earth?, vv. 4–11
   2. have you ever done or experienced. . . ?, vv. 12–18a
III. Interlude that strengthens the demand for a response
   1. answer if you "know" all this, v. 18b
   2. "do you know?" (where knowledge is clearly the basis for action), vv. 19–20
   3. ironic (?) exclamation, v. 21
IV. Further alternating do or can you?/who? questions
   1. do you know?, vv. 22–24
   2. who?, vv. 25–29
   3. can you . . . ?, vv. 31–35
   4. who?, vv. 36–38
   5. can you?, vv. 39–40
   6. who?, v. 41

This structure of the "sense" of this text with its insistent, repetitive "who?" points us beyond the text to its referential dimension, especially in the sense of a world governed by God which is the real world Job inhabits—or ought to acknowledge inhabiting. In this sense, it prepares us for Job's responses, though not exactly for either of them. I will pass over any attempt to comprehend why in his first response Job chooses silence (40:4–5) with its implication not only of awe, but also of absolute domination, to concentrate on the puzzle evoked by 42:5b. To the extent that my brief reading of Job 38 emphasizes the importance of the "who?" question, with its obvious answer, Job's failure to dwell upon the wonders he has "seen" in favor of a confession regarding Yahweh is made plausible. Yet the specific claim that he has "seen" God remains surprising. A logically sufficient response would have been "Yahweh" or "You, Yahweh." This surprise in the narrative of Job's vision whereby he not only acknowledges God, but also sees him is an addition that is not entirely ruled out by what goes before, yet it is certainly not predicted by it. So my understanding of this text, if my attempted application of Ricoeur's theory has any merit, retains an element of the paradoxical, a theological paradox regarding the structure of theophanies that the book of Job nowhere removes. In other words, to comprehend Job, it seems we must be able to comprehend how the appearance of something other than God can at the same time be the appearance of God.

A more definite result of such a reading is its calling into question the usual tendency to see this chapter of Job as focused on the facts of creation and providence. Job sees more than these, although it is not clear exactly what since the emphasis is on who rather than what is perceived or how such perception occurs. But that Yahweh is for the author of Job a necessary part of Job's life-world as well as the world he might more self-consciously inhabit seems obvious.

Whether such an analysis can resolve the difficult questions concerning how Yahweh's reponse settles the problems raised earlier in the book by Job and his companions regarding his condition, with their implication that either he or Yahweh must be righteous, but not both of them—something we know not to be the case from the opening prose portion of the text—must remain an open question, as must any general discussion of the relation of chapter 38 to the unity and continuity of the book as a whole.

My experience in applying Ricoeur's theory must end here. Let me note two more questions in closing, however, that arise from such an adventure when we return to the level of hermeneutical theory and reflection. My efforts have been based on what I have called Ricoeur's hermeneutical wager. They presuppose that Job 38 must have some meaning, a presupposition that characterizes even those theories Ricoeur has so ably discussed under the label of hermeneutics of suspicion. For Freud, as for Marx and Nietzsche, "texts" always have a meaning. It is just not what it seems to be or claims to be at first glance. My first question therefore, is whether hermeneutical theory can make a place for the possibility that a text may not have a meaning. Or that it may lose its meaning. I know that this is not Ricoeur's route. I am curious, however, whether we can specify under what conditions something can fail to make sense to us, a conclusion that, as itself intelligible, relies on another level of meaning, but not one I suspect that rules out this possibility.

Second, to return to the question concerning the status and role of approaches to texts, such as historical criticism, that are more inclined to ask what something meant rather than what it means, may we not say that a general theory of hermeneutics must both require their application in its explanatory phase and preserve their integrity as possible options in interpretation in their own right? That is, hermeneutics does not simply exclude inquiry for its own sake into what a text meant either in its original setting or at some period in the history of its transmission. We need not always ask what a text means for us, even while we recognize that such detours can add to and further clarify that meaning. (For Ricoeur's most complete discussion to date of this question, see 1971a.)

In return, Ricoeur's continued existential emphasis points to the need for a more adequate recognition of the situation of all such undertakings. Every attempt to specify what a text meant presupposes a contemporary point of view that needs to be more clearly acknowledged and analyzed insofar as it is a part of the subjective dimension of any hermeneutical theory. This would not be a move to a simple-minded assertion of relativism, rather it would be to make clear the wider conditions of intelligibility that make such assertions possible and that give them their own meaning.

WORKS CONSULTED

Dhorme, E.
1967 *A Commentary on the Book of Job.* London: Thomas Nelson and Sons.

Driver, S. R. and G. B. Grey
1921 *A Critical and Exegetical Commentary on the Book of Job Together With a New Translation.* Edinburgh: T. & T. Clark.

Glatzer, N., ed.
1969 *The Dimensions of Job: A Study and Selected Readings.* New York: Schocken Books.

Gordis, R.
1965 *The Book of God and Man.* Chicago: University of Chicago Press.

Kissane, E.
1939 *The Book of Job Translated from a Critically Revised Hebrew Text with Commentary.* Dublin: Browne and Nolan.

Lévêque, J.
1970 *Job et Son Dieu.* Paris: Librairie Lecoffre.

Polzin, R., and D. Robertson, eds.
1977 *Semeia* 7: "Studies in the Book of Job."

Pope, M. H.
1965 *Job.* Anchor Bible. Garden City, N.Y.: Doubleday.

Ricoeur, P.
1971a "Du conflit à la convergence des méthodes en exégèse biblique." Pp. 35–52 in *Exégèse et Herméneutique.* R. Barthes et al. Paris: Seuil.
1971b "The Model of the Text: Meaningful Action Considered as a Text." *Social Research* 38: 529–562.
1965 *History and Truth.* Evanston, IL: Northwestern University Press.
1973 "The Hermeneutical Function of Distanciation." *Philosophy Today* 17: 129–141.
1974 *The Conflict of Interpretations.* Evanston, IL: Northwestern University Press.
1975 "Biblical Hermeneutics." *Semeia* 4: 29–148.
1976 *Interpretation Theory: Discourse and the Surplus of Meaning.* Fort Worth: Texas Christian University Press.
1977a *The Rule of Metaphor.* Toronto: University of Toronto Press.
1977b "Writing as a Problem for Literary Criticism and Philosophical Hermeneutics." *Philosophic Exchange* 2:3–15.

Rowley, H. H.
1970 *Job.* London: Thomas Nelson & Sons.

Sanders, P. S., ed.
1968 *Twentieth Century Interpretation of the Book of Job*. Englewood Cliffs, NJ: Prentice-Hall.

Terrien, S.
1957 *Job: Poet of Existence*. Indianapolis, IN: Bobbs-Merrill.

von Rad, G.
1965 "Job XXXVIII and Ancient Egyptian Wisdom." Pp. 281–291 in *The Problem of the Hexateuch and Other Essays*. Edinburgh & London: Oliver & Boyd.
1972 *Wisdom in Israel*. Nashville, TN: Abingdon Press.

PART III
Discussion of the Preceding Essays

THE SENSE OF THE TEXT
AND A NEW VISION

Frederick J. Bolton
St. Olaf College

It seems to me that David Pellauer states something very important which is so often made too little of: that the history of comments on the book of Job exhibits more of the commentators than of the text itself as sense and reference. It has not been the allegorizers alone who used the text of Job for extrinsic intent. Clearly, subjectivity has not been methodically acknowledged. Neither, therefore, has the text been encountered in its own integrity. Modern focus on existential anguish as seen in the character of Job is not excluded here.

If I understand Ricoeur's theory at all, the central concern of the interpreter lies both in ascertaining the sense of the text, and beyond that to clarify something of how this text jars the existing subject into possession of a new subjectivity with a new vision of self, of selves, and of world. Such a miracle, however, involves the collision of past insight and formed concepts with new insight which mothers a movement towards altered concepts befitting new patterns of action and response in the human world.

David Pellauer correctly reminds us of the tentative nature of the text of this book. Nevertheless, as it stands, there is universal appeal and significance in the text. It is in its present form that it shocks us, and in this form that we too often try to tame it. What new vision does it open to the subject who struggles with just this text? What is the shock which requires that successive generations of commentators feel the need to struggle with it, and so reveal themselves to future generations?

It seems to me that in Job 38 we have the core of the shock. That shock lies precisely in the figurative shock presented by the whirlwind and the speech of the voice out of the whirlwind to Job. Here all subjectivity is aroused and forced into the open. Here, what has been formed in any era and comes to the text is put to test and into crisis. Only such a subjectivity in crisis can be a learning and receptive subjectivity.

Since it is the nature of the "who" questions and the "can you" questions that the answer to them is obvious, it seems not possible for these questions to be classified as merely "ironic," as many have suggested. Irony, after all, involves meaning as contrary to that seemingly expressed. Nor is there ground in the entire text of the book to speak of the questions as sarcastic or caustic since there is nothing ill-natured about them, unless all educational shock can be so judged. The very point of God's response to Job sets the mood otherwise.

The context is that Job has asked the question of how he is to be vindicated but has also set the line of his vindication in terms of the theology of God's equity, which claims to know what equitable sovereignty in human life might involve. The implication is that there is an answer in terms of that formula which God must give.

Explicit in these questions to Job, then, is a fresh look at God's creative rule so that he can be seen as knowing to do acts beyond the measure of Job's comprehension. Perspective is restored. Why is it irony to place Job's question in more adequate perspective? Job's conceptual tradition, brought to the encounter with God, is shocked purposefully.

Neither should these questions be classified as mockery or sarcasm. Is it not true that, as William Temple once said, the truest form of respect is even sometimes to resist another? Here God is presented in the text as resisting the questioner in precisely the only respectful and kind manner possible when a question is asked on the presumption that the questioner knows what he is asking. I agree with David Pellauer, therefore, that it would be near the truth to classify these speeches as a Socratic set of questions.

The point of this text seems to be that wisdom, not merely theoretical explanations and information, is required to deal with Job's concern. If indeed the sufferer's question is to be reframed and answered satisfactorily, the answer may be more than Job can handle.

God's questions are serious and imply: "Could you understand like one who could do thus? Are you able to bear the required answer? If you are able to deal with that answer, why would you need such an answer? Wouldn't you already possess what you request?" Here is no imagery of an Oriental despot, as in the prose prologue, nor is this an image of a celestial Principle of Equity giving no consideration of persons subjected to impersonal measures, as in the advice of the elders and in Job's thought. The ways of JHVH are not the ways comprehensible to the questioner working from current concepts.

However, Job does repent of his assumption that he can deal adequately with God and finite and pathetic existence in terms already familiar to him. God's resistance to Job's question does not, that is, negate Job or his efforts to possess wisdom, but only provides grounds to relativize Job's concepts and instigate their reformation.

The power of Job 38 in regard to the reader seems to consist in its direct address to any subject for which knowing and doing tend to become separated or for whom the images of God have become dead metaphors in tradition. For such a subject concepts of God tend toward the claim of comprehension and thus risk conceptual idolatry. It is such a consciousness that is shocked by the text and is thus given a new vision of theological faithfulness within integral personal faithfulness in life. The subject with a new vision of God which shatters conceptual tradition awakens to fascination with God's presence and wisdom and repents of the former claims of conceptual adequacy. Old root metaphors and concepts of God and of faithful man are offended and, for that very reason, the reading subject is opened to new possibilities. He is freed from the limits of his former and apparent wisdom so that his questions express serious curiosity and wonder rather than professional cynicism or self pity. The text of Job creates distance from the subjectivity brought to the text.

The speeches of God stress the fact that He knows how to care for all His creatures, whether or not man understands the ways of such care. We do not have a picture of God as Love, nor as the suffering God, nor the otherwise self-limiting God except for the more fundamental insight of the creature-affirming purpose of power which can best be figured, for the purposes of this text, as whirlwind vitality.

The book of Job raises issues as to the adequacy of theological concepts to comprehend sovereign rule in history, to explain fates, and to predict fortunes. It raises the issue of religious subjectivity itself as to the principles of its formation and reformation.

We see that God's speech, for all its display, does not leave Job cowed, but rather Job feels affirmed. Though he repents he shows no need to cease asking for wisdom. If he repents of his underlying assumption, that he would understand an explanation should he get it, the repentance does not seem to entail the abandonment of questions. What remains, then, is repentance of the assumption that he already held the terms of explanation and justification of God's ways—that Divine Wisdom could be justified in terms of his formula of just sovereignty. Truly, Job may be impelled now to ask questions in a search for better terms and deeper understanding. There is nothing in this book which shows God's speech to belittle Job (or humanity, if Job be taken allegorically).

The figure of a voice out of the whirlwind does not suggest stark terror or mere submission as the proper response of the vulnerable human, nor does it suggest easy familiarity with the ways of God in history or in human experience. The figure sets forth God's oft cheapened sovereignty in terms which will enlarge Job's readiness to observe and listen and reappraise what he hears and sees. Such sovereign display, at the same time, respects the Creature in us enough to address Job and so affirm his value, though Job had come to doubt that value and ask for death. The problem had always been his old theology whose honored root metaphors of blind equity cheapened Job by its terms for justification of majestic sovereignty.

The subjectivity of the interpreter is clarified by the text iself as it confronts him with the limit inherent in his own conceptuality, reasserts the noetic significance of live metaphor itself, and stimulates theological reconstruction. The book of Job uses the problem of suffering as occasion to test and awaken the subjectivity of the reader to itself.

As final comment, a most interesting feature of Mr. Pellauer's paper is his invitation to Ricoeur to clarify the conditions for failure of a text to have meaning. Possibly such clarification would make for greater precision with meaningful texts. In such development, one would want to know if there were more to be accounted for than loss of historical or psychic referents or the emptying of primary metaphors in the processes of time and cultural change. Possibly the history of transformations of the human self provides clues to such conditions. Exegesis probably begins on the assumption that every text meant something and still does. A superstitious approach to inscriptions is not of interest to Paul Ricoeur. The conditions of exegetical impossibility could point up important assumptions and concerns for critical theory.

THREE WAYS IN TEXT INTERPRETATION

Donald R. Buckey
Mount Union College

This response will comment on three ways of viewing and doing text interpretation, as exemplified in the essays of Michael Fox, David Pellauer, and André Lacocque.

1.   Michael Fox.

(a) Fox views the text as a vehicle of an author's meaning, as the means whereby he conveys *his* meaning. (b) He understands text interpretation as understanding the author's intended meaning (what he *meant*). This requires, first, a literary-historical study of the text, seeking to learn about the author and the original form of his meanings. Once this is completed, exegesis can begin, with understanding achieved when the propositional context of the text has been ascertained. (c) He grants that texts also have contemporary significance (what it *means*). The writer's meanings can be meaningful for later readers.

In regard to the elements of Ricoeur's theory that I have outlined in the Appendix at the end of this article, Fox's approach could be said to involve IB and IIA, with emphasis on the left side of the dialectic. The text is a source for discerning an author's intended meanings, which meanings involve both a situational reference and sense. The notion of the text's semantic autonomy is rejected. Interpretation itself involves describing the formal characteristics of the text ("explanation"?) and suggesting its propositional content ("understanding"?). The latter, in reference to Job 38, appears to be "God rules over nature and man."

I find Fox's actual exegesis to be creative and suggestive. Although he does not explicitly avail himself of Ricoeur's dialectic or accept Ricoeur's view of the independent power of the text, it appears to me that his exegesis of the meaning of Job 38 has surpassed the author of Job's intended meaning. (Whether this is the case we shall, of course, never know.)

Fox's rhetorical criticism is an explanatory technique that results in an enhanced appreciation of the sense of the text and a richer understanding of its significance (Ricoeur's "reference"). The result of this exegetical approach is that, as Fox notes, the reader is carried along with Job. I don't know about Job but I think Fox has illustrated Ricoeur's point about successful interpretation. Distanciation has been overcome and appropriation has occurred (" . . . interpretation actualizes the meaning of the text for the present reader," 1976:92). So perhaps in spite of himself, Fox has moved in an instructive fashion from answering the question "what it *meant*" to a consideration of "what it now *means*."

Each individual reader will have to decide whether Job 38 so construed has led to a new self-understanding—indeed, even more, whether it helps create a self (1976:94–95). Such claims probably appear extravagent to most contemporary historians. To give credence to such a claim requires a philosophical/theological commitment to the revealing and creative power of God (or Being). I shall have more on this issue following comments on Pellauer's paper.

2.   David Pellauer.

I find Pellauer's paper to be a lucid and helpful summary of Ricoeur's interpretive system, making reference to both sides of the dialectic I have labeled as IA, IB, and IIA.

In reading Job 38, Pellauer undertakes the twofold interpretive movement noted in IIA. The second movement, from explanation to understanding, results in the structure of Job 38 as outlined in his paper. This structure I find interesting, but not productive of the kind of comprehension Ricoeur claims should be the ideal outcome of such a structuralist kind of explanation.

Pellauer's critical reflection suggests he is aware that the comprehension that leads to appropriation has not been achieved here. He asks, as he concludes, "whether hermeneutical theory can make a place for the possibility that a text may *not* have a meaning?" (my italics). By "meaning" I take him to be referring to a presently *appropriable* meaning. I concur with his implied affirmative answer. Moreover, I agree with his further suggestion that a general theory of hermeneutic must allow a place for an inquiry which does not go beyond the quest for the "what it *meant*" of the text. While I have not found in Ricoeur any account of the legitimacy of excluding the "what does it *mean* for me" question from hermeneutics, a comment in *Interpretation Theory* appears to limit "world"-creating texts to those that one has "read, understood, and loved" (37). Indirectly this implies an exclusion.

I find it interesting that Pellauer, who brings to Job 38 a theory that should permit the overcoming of distanciation necessary for appropriation, does not appear (to me) to do so. Yet Fox, bereft of such a theory, succeeds. Is it not ironic that the former, who follows Ricoeur in the hermeneutical wager that an enduring text is always something to be interpreted and applied to any subsequent situation or context, loses the wager (again, in my judgment) while the latter, making no such wager, nevertheless achieves an "understanding (that) has less than ever to do with the author and his situation," one that succeeds in grasping "the world-propositions opened up by the reference of the text" (1976:87).

The question that interests me here is one occasioned by my reading of both Fox and Pellauer. It concerns Ricoeur's concept of "appropriation" (cf. IIB in Appendix). Is appropriation something that can publicly be discussed? How does it follow (logically, psychologically) from comprehension or understanding? Does its achievement require a *faith* commitment in the strong sense of a belief in YHWH and the possibilities of a new human being?

Loretta Dornisch claims that for Ricoeur's "believing is integrally related to interpreting" (1975:6). Does not this belief, present in the "second naïveté," go beyond the mere wager that a text is presently meaningful to include the belief in a hierophany of the sacred (Ricoeur, 1967:352)? How else are we to account for Ricoeur's claims listed under *appropriation* on my outline of *Interpretation Theory* (see Appendix)? In any case, I am interested in hearing how others view the relationship between Comprehension and Appropriation.

3. André Lacoque

Lacocque interprets the text and then views it. My first reading of his interpretation (Section I) led me to exclaim, "No, he's got it all wrong." While I was impressed with his learned exegesis, my own reading of Job 38 and the standard commentaries led me to conclude that this was a fine example of the "fruitful misunderstanding" mentioned by Fox. Various Protestant commitments have led to an eisegesis of Job that falsely opposes nature to history, religion to faith. Surely Robert Gordis is right in claiming that the "identification of the God of history *and of nature* is steadfastly maintained in . . . the Speeches of the Lord Out of the Whirlwind. Neither Job . . . nor God himself is able or willing to 'solve' the problem of evil by making a dichotomy between nature and history, between the natural order and the moral order" (1978:561, my italics).

But after a careful study of his reflections upon his interpretation (Section II) and a look at *Semeia* 4, I'm not sure my initial judgment was correct. That is, after viewing Lacoque's interpretation in light of Ricoeur's theory, I am led to admit that Lacoque's reading of Job 38 may be a permissible one—if Ricoeur's theory is sound.

In viewing the Job text as metaphoric, in regarding YHWH as a controlling symbol and qualifier, in taking the inexplicable suffering of man as a limit-experience, Lacoque can make a Ricoeurian case for his claim that Job is about "the impotence of religion and philosophy." In emphasizing the right rather than the left side of the dialectic (see Appendix), a good argument is made for a reading of Job that goes beyond the standard interpretations. Whatever the original author meant (utterer's meaning), the reference of the *utterance meaning* transgresses the original meaning, and Lacoque has shown that the surplus of meaning in the symbolic Job has to do with a God who suffers with us and not with a God of retribution.

Do we have an appropriable meaning? Perhaps. In the light of the Holocaust (one source of our contemporary meaningless *Umwelt*) the God who suffers with us may help create a *Welt* for us, an endurable—because intelligible—world. The existence of a powerless God who is nevertheless still God can—thanks to Job—empower us to exclaim, like Job, "Though He slay me, yet I trust in Him" (Job 13:15).

The question these reflections on Lacoque's paper raise for me is this. What relationship in text interpretation does the "what it *meant*" dimension have to the "what it *means*" dimension? Ricoeur talks about the historical-critically determined interpretation having a "kind of priority and ... controlling" function in text interpretation (1975:134). Does it? Must it? If the answer to these questions is "yes," can Lacoque's interpretation be legitimate? (Let us assume for the sake of discussion that his Section I exegesis of Job 38 has not been convincing.)

WORKS CONSULTED

Dornisch, Loretta
1975   "Symbolic Systems and the Interpretation of Scripture: An Introduction to the Work of Paul Ricoeur." *Semeia* 4:1–21.

Gordis, Robert
1978   *The Book of Job*. New York: The Jewish Theological Seminary of America.

Ricoeur, Paul
1967   *The Symbolism of Evil*. Boston: Beacon Press.
1975   "Biblical Hermeneutics." *Semeia* 4:27–148.
1976   *Interpretation Theory: Discourse and the Surplus of Meaning*. Fort Worth: Texas Christian University Press.

Appendix
Schema of Paul Ricoeur's *Interpretation Theory* (1976)

Human Being in World (experiencing Power)

I. THEORY OF DISCOURSE
(Bringing Experience to Language)

Discourse (oral) — Going Public / self-expression

A. *Speaking*

- actualized as → EVENT (of speech) (Bios)
  - Utterer's Meaning
  - SENSE & Reference (situational) the "What," propositional content

- understood as → MEANING (of expression) (Logos)
  - Utterance Meaning
  - Sense & REFERENCE (nonostensive) the "About What," points beyond text to a world

Speaker ⟶ Message ⟶ Hearer

B. *Writing*

Author's Meaning — Inscription Symbolic Expression — Semantic Autonomy Surplus of Meaning

II. INTERPRETATION THEORY (re. *Reading*)
(Bringing Language to Experience)

A. *Understanding Discourse*
   (Semantic Dimension)

```
                          Text as Work
       EXPLANATION ←─────────────────────→ UNDERSTANDING

1st Step              parts to whole
       validation ─────────────────────→ guess
                  (counterpart of dialectic
                   between event and meaning)

2nd Step              depicting structures
       explanation ───────────────────→ comprehension
                  (counterpart of dialectic
                   between sense and reference)
```

B. *Appropriating Discourse*
   (Existential
   Dimension)

DISTANCIATION   APPROPRIATION

                                           Power of Disclosing Word
                                           —basis for "new mode of being"
                                                     "realizing a self"
                                           NEW EVENT

SPEECH AND SILENCE IN JOB

Robert Paul Dunn
Loma Linda University

All the essays are concerned with propositional meaning, but Michael Fox's paper suggests most strongly that the meaning of the text, which is for him the authorial intention, is clearly demonstrated by its written form. It is a well argued, conservative defense of a literalist reading of the passage of Job. It consciously proposes a more extreme position on semantic autonomy than does Ricoeur, who rejects the "fallacy of the absolute text" in *Interpretation Theory*, even though Ricoeur, too, looks on the text as central in interpretation. In his first footnote Fox asks, concerning Ricoeur, "If inscription does indeed entail 'disconnection of the mental intention of the author from the verbal meaning of the text, of what the author meant and what the text means,' then does not authorial meaning become merely a historical datum which has no greater relevance to the text's meaning than does the interpretation of each and every reader?"

Fox's concern for both authorship and meaning is important, yet one wonders just how far it will take us in that dialectic between "explanation" and "understanding" that Ricoeur sees as the heart of interpretation. His concern would seem to relate more to the explanatory pole of interpretation than to the understanding. First, his concern for authorship seems basically an editorial one—the recovery of the authentic text. This is the task of the textual scholar, and it is one that can be achieved through the science of historical and analytical bibliography. Second, his concern for meaning, which takes over once the authentic text has been recovered, is essentially formalist and preoccupied with propositional content. In particular his analysis of the text's rhetorical questions is helpful, especially when he suggests that these questions help to establish "a special intimacy of communication" between Job/reader and God/author. Yet the vision of meaning given to Job and the reader does not appear basically new, but rather an explanation of what they have already known. In Fox's paraphrase God sounds like a weary schoolteacher: "You know very well that I and I alone created order and maintain it in the world, and I know that you know, and you know that I know that you know. This is the meaning of God's opening challenge."

Although it stresses (as all rationalist readings of Job eventually must) the justice and authority of God, this reading is not one that we would wish to fault totally. In particular, in its insistence that the interpreter ought to emphasize more the techniques of historical and analytical bibliography, it does a real service. Even though Ricoeur has himself extolled the virtue of the "long route" through the scientific or quasi-scientific disciplines of modern scholarship over Heidegger's "shorter route" to meaning by a process of intuition, he does not stress very much the importance of ascertaining the reading of the text. He rather seems to assume that this has been done without questioning it for himself. Fox shows rather graphically the importance of not forgetting to do this.

Yet Fox's reading is incomplete: it does well at explaining the text, but it fails to help us to achieve a new understanding. How are we to get beyond our imprisonment within the text seen as a propositional document? Here is where Paul Ricoeur is useful. At the end of *Interpretation Theory*, Ricoeur goes beyond the cognitive and explanatory emphasis of "sense" analysis to wrestle with the difficulty of specifying the non-linguistic aspects of "reference." As David Pellauer suggests, even here the emphasis in Ricoeur is on positive meaning: the assumption is always that the text can tell us *something*. Yet Ricoeur realizes that what the text tells is not always of a verbal nature. Consequently Ricoeur seems to move to new levels of meaning; the text does not remain on the same level. In the interpretation of a text as challenging and difficult as Job, this is extremely important.

Professor Lacocque sees this clearly in his paper. From the beginning he shows that it is inadequate to see God as merely overwhelming Job by the force of his rhetoric so that Job is forced into silence. The virtue of Lacocque's paper is that it moves beyond the rationalist gods of surrounding nations, who are locked into nature and into "philosophical" or "religious" discourse, and into the world of *Yhwh*, which is no longer purely verbal but social and historical. Thus both Job and God are led into the silence of discourse, a silence that is created not so much by God's "victory" in a dispute as by Job and God entering into a new relationship. This, at any rate, is how I would interpret Lacocque's last paragraph about "the total collapse of meaning," for when God "speaks" in the whirlwind it is not to explain any religious or philosophical *aporia*, but to come near to Job as one living being to another.

However, Lacocque leaves unexplored the nature of this aspect that deserves further consideration in interpretation theory. It would seem that a discussion of this positive silence might answer, or at least help to answer, one of Pellauer's two concluding questions in his paper: "Whether hermeneutical theory can make a place for the possibility that a text may not have a meaning?" As an English teacher I am inclined to answer yes and, in support of this position, to show the latest stack of freshman themes! But clearly this failure of expression is not what Pellauer means. Nor does he quite mean what I am going to suggest either. It is impossible to discuss fully his challenging question in this response. What I would suggest is that interpretation theory has been too exclusively concerned with propositional meaning. Discourse not only satisfies the human need for meaning, but it also provides us with such non-cognitive benefits as beauty—including rhythm, figurative language, and melody—and a sense of what Fox calls "a special intimacy." Probably Pellauer has something more negative in mind than this; nevertheless, this does point to the possibility of a certain silence or absence of meaning if by "meaning" one means what it seems to mean in the papers we are considering, i.e., propositional meaning. I do not mean to say here that this beauty and intimacy cannot indicate propositional meaning, too. My point is merely that they go far beyond that, so that (as in Job) we arrive at a point where speech gives way to silence.

This silence of which I speak is located "beyond" propositional meaning. However, I do not mean a silence that is beyond speech in the sense that it is in Eastern religions, where ultimate reality is seen as nonverbal and the verbal is relegated to *samsaric* or illusory existence. The silence I speak of is only beyond propositional speech; it is not beyond discourse. Rather this silence is within the very heart of discourse.

Since this is a response rather than a full-length paper, I shall not be able to begin to detail to any extent the forms and functions of such silence in discourse generally nor in Job in particular. I do, however, wish to underscore the need of interpretation theory to come to grips with this factor by another comment or two. Language itself, it has been said, comes out of silence and returns to silence /1/. That silence may be seen as either "full" or "empty," depending upon the orientation of the author considered. The attitude of the interpreter may sometimes also be crucial. Paul Ricoeur prefers a dialectic between the two. It is possible to see over the course of his recent writings the development of this dialectic between speech and silence and between what I would term an "empty" and a "full" silence. *The Symbolism of*

Evil demonstrates as well as any work I know how language is born in certain crisis situations as a way of responding to and symbolizing the empty, meaningless, and baffling silence of human chaos, as a way of providing a sense of order. In *Freud and Philosophy* he redefined his understanding of symbolic speech to include all multi-vocal expressions arising out of existential crises. But he still has to explore more fully than he has yet done how symbolic speech leads to a potentially "full" silence, a silence that is productive but that is far more than propositional utterance. This he has only begun to do in *Interpretation Theory*.

This silence is not the absence, failure, or even inadequacy of words. Such a silence may be characteristic of Eastern literature and of some Western writing, such as that of Beckett. But it is not the main tradition of our culture, nor the orientation of Ricoeur. Further, this silence is not emotional; it does not depend on the subjective attitude of the reader. Whether this silence presents a "fullness" or an "emptiness" of being, it is mediated to the reader by the author and the text. This silence—and this point may be a useful supplement to Fox's paper—is a silence that returns us to the author on another level. (This movement to another level is less apparent if the silence is "empty" than if it is "full" and "present," but I would argue that there is still a difference between the silence of primordial chaos, which is simply confused, and the silence experienced at the end of a *Waiting for Godot*, which is stark and clear). In terms of the dialectic between distanciation and appropriation that characterizes the modern interpretation theory that we are interested in, the text first of all separates us from the author through the process of inscription; but then it gives us back a sense of the author again in the movement from internal sense to exterior reference. The loss of physical author in writing is, in one sense, a great blow, but he cannot be recovered simply through intentional or editorial analysis. Then we would only have a spiritual recovery of the author as a full person constituted by both body and spirit. The text, through its rhythm, figurative language, and melody, cannot, of course, miraculously give us the living author, but it does direct us to a realm of silence in which we commune with him in a transformed way. But the text also, as Ricoeur would emphasize, gives us the world anew—we are not simply limited to the author and perhaps at the end we are not even very conscious of him.

If I had time I would comment on how direct statement, metaphor, symbol, negative or ironic statement, and simple silence itself can help us to understand discourse more fully than propositional analysis alone can do. But since there is not time for this, let me simply suggest that a significant beginning in this direction has been made by Mary Anne McPherson Oliver, in an essay entitled "Mystical Experience and the Literary Technique of Silence," in *Studia Mystica*,

1:1 (Spring 1978), 5-20. This analysis would be interesting to apply to the passage in Job, for it would help us to experience more fully and concretely the relation between God and Job. The irony, the humor, the questions, the metaphors or symbols all go beyond rational discourse. And even the silence at the end of the dialogue is the silence of presence, of assent and communion, rather than of defeat.

NOTE

/1/   Michele Federico Sciacca is quoted in Ambrose G. Wathen, OSB, *Silence: The Meaning of Silence in the Rule of St. Benedict* (Washington, D.C.: Cistercian Publications/Consortium Press, 1973), p. xii.

The Chicago Society of Biblical Research announces publication of BIBLICAL RESEARCH in a double issue, volumes XXIV–XXV (1979–1980)

SYMPOSIUM: PAUL RICOEUR AND BIBLICAL HERMENEUTICS

Contents:

"Job and the Symbolism of Evil" — by André Lacocque

"Paradox Gives Rise to Metaphor: Paul Ricoeur's Hermeneutics and The Parables of Jesus" — by John Dominic Crossan

"Paul Ricoeur on Biblical Interpretation" — Lewis S. Mudge

"A Response" — by Paul Ricoeur

Price $6.00 prepaid

Address orders to:
Biblical Research
5555 So. Woodlawn Avenue
Chicago, Illinois 60637

New from Scholars Press Titles from THE SOCIETY OF BIBLICAL LITERATURE

Joanna Dewey
Markan Public Debate: Literary Technique, Concentric Structure and Theology in Mark 2:1–3:6

Markan Public Debate: This dissertation is a rhetorical analysis—the study of literary technique and surface structure—of Mark 2:1–3:6.

Price: Cloth, $12.00 (8.00); paper, $7.50 (5.00)
SP Code: 06 01 48
SBL DISSERTATION SERIES

Rifat Sonsino
Motive Clauses in Hebrew Law: Biblical Forms and Near Eastern Parallels

This study, utilizing form-critical methodology, analyzes the motive clauses in the Pentateuchal legal corpora in light of Biblical and extra-Biblical literature. The author discusses the form and setting of Biblical and cuneiform laws and the form, function and originality of the motive clauses.

Price: Cloth, $13.50 (9.00); paper, $9.00 (6.00)
SP Code: 06 01 45
SBL DISSERTATION SERIES

Charles W. Hedrick
The Apocalypse of Adam: A Literary and Source Analysis

The book identifies and discusses two sources that were edited in antiquity in order to form the present version of the *Apocalypse of Adam*.

Price: Cloth, $15.00 (10.00); paper, $10.50 (7.00)
SP Code: 06 01 46
SBL DISSERTATION SERIES

David J. Lull
The Spirit in Galatia: Paul's Interpretation of Pneuma as Divine Power

Today, a Process perspective, in dialogue with Bultmann's and Pannenberg's interpretations of the Spirit in Paul's theology. This work helps to develop a concept of the Spirit as the divine power of creative transformation.

Price: Cloth, $13.50 (9.00); paper $9.00 (6.00)
SP Code: 06 01 49
SBL DISSERTATION SERIES

J. T. Forestell C.S.B.
Targumic Traditions and the New Testament: An Annotated Bibliography with a New Testament Index

A bibliographical survey of recent literature which utilizes the traditions contained in the Targums for the elucidation of New Testament texts. The work is designed as a handy reference tool for New Testament scholars.

Price: Cloth, $16.50 (11.00); paper, $12.00 (8.00)
SP Code: 06 13 04
SBL ARAMAIC STUDIES

Israel Yeivin, E. J. Revell, translator
Introduction to the Tiberian Masorah

This book provides basic information on all features of the Tiberian Masorah, from a description of the most important manuscripts of the Hebrew Bible to an explanation—with many examples—of the standard terms used in their notes.

Price: Paper only, $10.50 (7.00)
SP Code: 06 05 05
SBL MASORETIC SERIES

Scholars Press, 101 Salem Street, P.O. Box 2268, Chico, CA 95927

COSMOS AND COVENANT

Walter James Lowe
Emory University

I shall attempt to cast some light upon Ricoeur's interpretation theory by turning to his interpretive practice, specifically his discussion of Job in *The Symbolism of Evil*, and by comparing Ricoeur's conclusions to those of the very helpful paper given us by André Lacocque.

Let me begin by proposing a simple typology. Discussions of the voice from the whirlwind may emphasize either what God says or the fact *that* God speaks: they may stress the response or the responding, the content or the act. Central to the first reading of Job will be the panoramic survey of creation; let us call it the *cosmic* approach. Central to the second reading is the fact of Job's being addressed and the relationship which is thereby established or confirmed; let us call it the *dialogic* approach.

We may now ask whether Ricoeur gravitates toward one or another side of this distinction. I wish to say immediately that typologies are made to be transgressed and that it is not my intent to compartmentalize Ricoeur; but the reader of the section of *The Symbolism of Evil* on "The Reaffirmation of the Tragic" may well be struck by the extent to which the author seems to compartmentalize himself. For as Lacocque observes, "Ricoeur sees the response of Job in the last chapters as a submission to the *tragic*, for he converts freedom and necessity into *fate*, thus triumphing over the ethical vision of the world" (see Ricoeur, 1967:321). And for Ricoeur the source of this tragic resignation is precisely what we have characterized as the cosmic approach: it arises from "the contemplation of the whole" (321).

Conversely Ricoeur is equally explicit that the answer has little to do with personal address: "There is nothing in the revelation that concerns him personally . . ."/1/. Indeed, so emphatic is Ricoeur in this regard that he portrays Job as being able to initiate the crucial, tragic insight on the basis of the very *absence* of God. "Faced with the torturing absence of God (23:8; 30:20), the man dreams of his own absence and repose: 'Henceforth I shall be invisible to every eye; your eyes shall be upon me and I shall have vanished' (7:8). Is it not the tragic God that Job discovers again? the inscrutable God of terror?" (319). In substance the determinative point may have been grasped before God ever speaks—so far has the answer been disengaged from the answering.

Now why is it that Ricoeur opts so emphatically for the cosmic approach? We must begin with the fact that Ricoeur reads the book as a dramatic refutation of the theory of retribution, a confounding of the ethical view of the world. This refutation is at work not only in the denunciation of Job's friends but in Job's own repentance as well. "It becomes suddenly apparent that the demand for retribution animated Job's recriminations no less than the moralizing homilies of his friends. That, perhaps, is why the innocent Job, the upright Job, repents" (321). The point at issue here is a certain anthropocentrism. The theory of retribution is, as Lacocque observes, an all-too-human scheme of things; and Ricoeur argues elsewhere that the ethical view of the world is an effort to define right and wrong almost exclusively in terms of the exercise of human freedom (1974:300). Such concentration upon the human entails, in Ricoeur's view, a premature cloture which is the endemic temptation of human reflection. Already at the time of *Freedom and Nature* Ricoeur insisted that "the Ego must more radically renounce the covert claim of all consciousness, must abandon its wish to posit itself, so that it can receive the nourishing and inspiring spontaneity which breaks the sterile circle of the self's constant return to itself" (1966:14).

Thus the significance of tragedy, and specifically of the cosmic approach to Job, springs from the fact that it breaks open this self-enclosing circle. The sweep of the cosmos—"inscrutable order, measure beyond measure"— dissolves the human pretention "to form by oneself a little island of meaning in the universe, an empire within an empire" (1967:321). Indeed Ricoeur's treatment of Job may be said to epitomize the argument which gave rise to *The Symbolism of Evil* in the first place; for his very turn to hermeneutics represented an effort to surmount the premises of a certain phenomenology (1974: 287–88; Ihde: 18–20). This hermeneutical birthright determines many of the most characteristically Ricoeurian themes of *The Symbolism of Evil*: the resilience of the symbol of stain, the unresolvability of the figure of the serpent and finally the irreducibility of the cycle of myths itself—which is characterized, quite fittingly, as "the reaffirmation of the tragic."

These remarks lead directly to the principal reservation which I have to express regarding Ricoeur's very illuminating exposition. Might it be that the strength of Ricoeur's concern at this point, regarding tragedy and the cosmic view, has led him to neglect another equally crucial feature of the text: namely its implicit context of covenant and dialogue? To be sure, Ricoeur does underline this context at one point; he cautions that "we must never lose sight of the fact that Job's plaint, even when it seems to be destroying the basis for any dialogal relation between God and man, does not cease to move in the field of invocation. It is to God that Job appeals against God" (1967:319). But the fact remains that for Ricoeur the tragic vision, which he adopts as the key to the meaning of Job, has already been suggested before God speaks; and that the character of that vision, after God has spoken, remains such as to permit unqualified comparison with such extrabiblical sources as Anaximander and Heraclitus (1967:321). Of course I am aware that one cannot assume *a priori* that the covenantal tradition, in any of its forms, is necessarily determinative for a particular Old Testament text. But the achievement of André Lacocque's paper, it seems to me, is to have demonstrated just such a connection in the present case, particularly as regards the name of YHWH. It is the importance of this context—the importance of the fact *that* God speaks at *all*—which is strangely absent from Ricoeur's account.

Now what does this cursory examination of Ricoeur's actual practice suggest regarding his interpretation theory? I will offer some brief remarks which are intended simply as possible topics for further discussion. (1) Ricoeur reinserts the tragic vision into the cycle of myths Specifically, the tragic vision "contributes to the understanding of" the Adamic myth (1967:322). In a sense it provides a propaedeutic to a right comprehension of that myth. (2) How does it do so? In part, I think, through its very *form*: for there is a form to the tragic vision consisting of a first moment of perplexity and scandal followed by a second moment of altered perspective and illumination which entails a new vision of the world. (3) A similar form is apparent in Ricoeur's recent treatment of the parables of the New Testament. Here too there is scandal, illumination and altered world and here too we find a sort of propaedeutic: the form itself is a clue to what the biblical witness is about. Such similarities of function and form suggest that at this point we touch upon certain features which are characteristic of Ricoeur's method as such. (4) Now I would submit that these features are significantly indebted to a specific philosophic tradition, namely that of German idealism. Indeed it may be argued that, despite the reservations indicated earlier, Ricoeur's hermeneutic continues to operate within a broadly phenomenological framework which derives from that tradition. But, at the same time, German idealism in certain of its aspects is the obvious archetype of all that Ricoeur would oppose, namely "the circle of the self's constant return to itself." This generates within Ricoeur's thought a very fundamental tension — one of which he is well aware and which he seeks to address through his repeated insistence upon the necessity of "distanciation" (e.g., 1976:25). Ricoeur's frequent methodological "detours" are, in effect, so many efforts to forestall the idealist cloture which certain other of his premises seem to invite. The question then becomes one of determining whether the efforts succeed — of judging whether there is sufficient distance in the distanciation. That question can be answered only in the concrete, and that is why the present discussion of Ricoeur's practice is so apposite. (5) A case in point is provided by our original typology. A number of philosophers such as Buber, Marcel, and Levinas have charged that the idealist tradition fails precisely at the point of recognizing the reality of encounter and dialogue. Without proposing an uncritical endorsement of any of these alternative philosophies, I would adopt them as background to a concluding question. Could it be that the eclipsing of the dialogic aspect in Ricoeur's reading of Job is no happenstance, but reflects a certain "idealist" bias which, despite his own best efforts, continues to affect his method /2/?

An adequate consideration of this question would undoubtedly lead one into a review of the entirety of Ricoeur's pilgrimage since the time of *The Symbolism of Evil* /3/. For the present I hope to have indicated that while the disagreement between Ricoeur and Lacocque over the nature of tragedy may be a matter of definition and while they exhibit an important agreement in seeing Job as the refutation of any complacent theory of retribution, still there exists between their readings of the text a substantive issue — an issue which has implications for the theory of interpretation as well.

NOTES

/1/ Ricoeur might be seen as suggesting a form of indirect address when he adds, "But precisely because it is not a question of himself, Job is challenged" (321).

/2/ In effect the question reflects a renewed appreciation of the difficulty (and the value) of the programmatic task Ricoeur set for himself at the begining of his *Philosophy of the Will*, namely to apply the rigor of Husserl's phenomenological method to the richness of Marcel's poetic meditations without betraying the spirit of either mentor (1966:15).

/3/ For a proposal regarding the issues at stake in one strand of Ricoeur's development, his treatment of psychoanalysis, see Lowe: 1979.

WORKS CONSULTED

Buber, Martin
    1970   *I and Thou*. New York: Scribners.

Ihde, Don
    1971   *Hermeneutic Phenomenology: The Philosophy of Paul Ricoeur*, Evanston, IL: Northwestern University Press.

Levinas, Emmanuel
    1969   *Totality and Infinity*. Pittsburgh, PA: Duquesne University Press.

Lowe, Walter
    1979   "Psychoanalysis and Humanism: The Permutations of Method." *JAAR* XLVII/1 Supplement (March): 135-69.

Marcel, Gabriel
    1952   *Metaphysical Journal*. Chicago: Regnery.

Ricoeur, Paul
    1966   *Freedom and Nature*. Evanston, IL: Northwestern University Press.
    1967   *The Symbolism of Evil*. New York: Harper and Row.
    1974   *The Conflict of Interpretations*. Evanston, IL: Northwestern University Press.
    1975   "Biblical Hermeneutics." *Semeia* 4: 27-148.
    1976   *Interpretation Theory: Discourse and the Surplus of Meaning*. Fort Worth: Texas Christian University Press.

THE *SILENCE* OF JOB AS THE KEY TO THE TEXT

Alan M. Olson
Boston University

I too come to this very difficult text in the book of Job as a philosopher-theologian and not as one carefully trained in the literary-exegetical sciences. Therefore, I will limit my comments to two aspects of Pellauer's paper, ignoring several of the very interesting questions he raises but which I am not able to explore with any authority.

My first series of comments has to do with the problem of "applying" hermeneutic philosophy to the task of interpreting a given text. This is what we have been asked to do with respect to Job 38 and Pellauer himself is cautious in the face of this task as evidenced by the number and kinds of questions he raises. It has always been my notion that what Ricoeur offers as being most valuable (and here I would also include Gadamer) does not have to do with the providing of specific methodological clues as to how the historical-critical-literary sciences might better go about their highly specialized tasks. What hermeneutic philosophy offers is a theory of understanding through which one might find a better way to integrate what the literary and exegetical sciences provide through their respective analyses. By the term "integrate" what I mean is the integration or self-appropriation of meaning by the individual, and not formal integration in the sense of the development of a wholly comprehensive discipline of interpretation that I see implied in Pellauer's notion of a "general hermeneutical theory."

To be sure Ricoeur of late has extended and refined his hermeneutic phenomenology through very impressive ventures into structuralism, philosophy of language, with the development of very specific theories of the text, including genre, style, sense and reference, metaphorical truth, and so forth. This latest highly technical work of Ricoeur—impresive as it is and surpassing by a considerable degree the work of others in the same general field—seems to me motivated not only by the desire to understand better the empirical contents of his own position, but may also be viewed as the means of obtaining the attention of scholars who have bracketed indefinitely the more cosmic concerns of theology and philosophy. Ricoeur wants to be taken seriously and in order to be taken seriously one must understand one's opponents at least as well as they understand themselves.

Now this, to me, is an admirable strategy and there are few who can handle the mediating task as well as Ricoeur. Indeed, "mediation," as Pellauer points out, is a definitive part of Ricoeur's hermeneutics. Nevertheless, the mediating task is not an easy one as Tillich and others have found out. It is difficult to have it both ways and I suspect this problem will continue in the future whatever new resources may be found in the development of new epistemological and ontological theories. Therefore, I can understand very well the force of Pellauer's implied criticism of Ricoeur's interpretation theory as containing certain elements that are still too subjectivistic and existentialistic. Certainly Ricoeur himself has tried to adumbrate these features in his more recent work, especially in his comments on conceptual mediation. The personal element, however, cannot be outstripped altogether if Ricoeur is to remain true to the basic direction of a life work that includes, we should not forget, a rather detailed exposition of aspects of the book of Job in *The Symbolism of Evil*. It will be recalled that in this work Ricoeur's purpose is decidedly personal, that is, Job is viewed as a means of "reappropriating the tragic" after having cast his wager for the Adamic myth as "the anthropological myth par excellence." That this work should have been criticized by many for being too Western, too Christian, and therefore too narrow and too apologetical is not surprising, nor is it, for me, objectionable unless one believes that it is somehow possible to obtain a definitive hold of both the "sense" and the "reference" of texts like Job. But Job is significant for me theologically and ontologically precisely because the questions of "sense" and especially "reference" are themselves shattered by the text much in the manner that all "ethical systems" are "shattered," as Ricoeur himself observes. This brings me to my second series of comments.

Together with his structural analysis of the text, Pellauer's commentary may be viewed as being informed by Ricoeur's attempt to rehabilitate Frege's distinctions concerning "sense" or what a text says and how it says it and "reference" or the meaning of what is said. Pellauer rightly points out that in the scriptures there are few cases where the "sense" of a text is more scrambled and confused than in the book of Job. The same may be said of the matter of "reference" and what the text finally means. Perhaps this is the reason why Pellauer raises the question as to "whether hermeneutical theory can make a place for the possibility that a text may not have a meaning"; in other words, when "effacement" and "distanciation" between the worlds of the text and reader are so absolute that they cannot be overcome a text may be meaningless. This is an interesting question but one that would have to be pursued on a case by case basis. In the book of Job we have a unique and potentially illuminating case.

Pellauer indicates, as do most commentators, that Job 38 turns on the questions of subject and object; the subject being framed by the question "who?" and the object being "what do you know?" with the implication that "if you know, then tell me!" The great feature of the text, of course, is that it drives both Job and the reader beyond knowledge ordinarily conceived as does no other text in the scriptures. What is at issue, however, is not merely the formal knowledge pertaining to theodicy but even more the kind of knowledge that is based upon personal intimate experience. Job is the "apple of God's eye," so to speak, and as such he is presented as a kind of human prototype or "second Adam" that may be viewed and understood strictly within and not external to the main body of Jewish tradition (and here in contrast to the Christ as the "second Adam" of Saint Paul). Thus to understand Job, we are faced not with the problems of an ordinary but an experiential "knower," one whose knowledge is conditioned by intimate position and privileged perspective of God's purpose, design, morality and justice. Job's knowledge does not derive, as in the case of his so-called friends, from merely knowing the "letter" of the Law but also its "spirit." Therefore Job, it would seem, is justifiably convinced that his predicament cannot be the product of divine causality for up to this point there is no "distanciation" whatsoever between himself and God; indeed, Job may be viewed as the exception to the conventions of ritual distanciation for he alone has been blessed by God beyond all others.

To state the matter another way one could say that Job is portrayed as the "master of both sense and reference"! Both Job and his friends seem to be equally aware of the "sense" of the Law, but they differ as to its "reference" or meaning. This hiatus is informed precisely by the fact that Job's knowledge is personal in addition to being formal. For this reason their counsel, well-reasoned as it is, is disregarded by Job. It is the discourse with Elihu that establishes this epistemological distinction preparing the way for what is to come beginning with Job 38, namely, that "all knowledge" of the Divine is a "conceit," even—and perhaps especially—the knowledge one assumes to have on the basis of pious personal experience. The imagery showered upon Job by God out to the theophany of the Whirlwind extends and compounds the fate of being "fallen" and finite far beyond what we find in the Adamic context. The Job we meet is not merely exiled to a more difficult but not altogether unreasonable existence because of transgression against the Law. He is a man utterly beaten into submission and "dominated," as Pellauer rightly observes, by a very unpleasant deity, precisely because he has assumed himself to be what I have termed the "master of reference."

And so we come to the "silence" of Job—and here I will discount its aftermath and especially 42:7—9, since emendations and redactions motivated by the pious concern of the cultus are not unknown to the Scriptures! How can Job's response be otherwise in the face of such a terrifying deity? One does not answer back to an absolute and only partially enlightened despot. And yet, it is precisely within and through "silence" that Job "sees." "What" Job sees, as Pellauer points out, is not at all clear; merely "that" he sees, and that this seeing leads to a kind of self-mortification and repentence. Because this is the case, that is, because the matter of "reference" is still confused, Pellauer suggests that the element of the "paradoxical" must be preserved since Job's experience does nothing to "remove" or to clarify the ambiguity inherent to biblical theophanies.

The word "paradoxical," it seems to me, is too weak a term in this context for the paradoxical still has logical properties. In the matter of Job's silence we are driven to the brink of the void if not directly into it, for the meaning of reference is eclipsed and annihilated. We are confronted, it would seem, by a genre of literature that goes beyond the tragic, for there is nothing to be appropriated by way of the kind of aesthetic conversion through empathetic participation that is characteristic of tragic wisdom. What Job "sees" is a reality the meaning of which utterly fails in the face of the limited possibilities of language—even poetic language, although Heidegger has made it clear that poetical speaking comes the closest since it is the most sensitive to the meaning of the "unspoken" and the "unspeakable," to the "is" that rises "where the word leaves off."

Having here just cited "the meaning of the unspoken" or "silence," I realize that the referential component of discourse has just been invoked. But I do not invoke it as a clue to be elucidated through some kind of conceptually based positive dialectics. I speak of reference here only in terms of the negative dialectics that is associated with the more sublime examples of Western mysticism and with Buddhist philosophy generally. Indeed, these are traditions that have insisted historically that the experience of *unio mystica* or *Nirvana* cannot take place apart from the *overcoming* of questions of sense and reference. And note that here I say "experience" and not "knowledge" of Ultimate Reality, for cognition is still captive to one or another of the forms of the *ego cogito cogitatum* referential models of knowledge and meaning to which Pellauer refers. The kind of experience to which I allude here no longer has to do with questions of reference. Objectifying thinking and all of its modalities has been left behind. That Job "sees" is all that can be said; "what" he sees cannot be said, for "to utter a word," as Plotinus once put it, is "to introduce deficiency," that deficiency being precisely the problem of reference. The best one can do, at second hand, so to speak, is to say with Tillich that Job here experiences "the fragmentary but unambiguous vision of the Unity of Being," or with Heidegger, and perhaps less pretentiously, that Job has come "into the neighborhood of Being." Such utterances are "doxological" or religious forms of speaking, as both Gadamer and Pannenberg have indicated, and are to be distinguished categorically from other kinds of speaking where the problem of reference can be raised less problematically. The rhetoric of Job's response and repentence, just as the "Fire" utterance of Pascal, may be perceived doxologically for they are conventionally apropos. "Even then," as Jaspers puts it, "it is as though one were saying nothing!"

Perhaps the ultimate lesson to be learned from hermeneutic philosophy is that when one is dealing with eminent texts that explore and bear witness to the hazardous domain of the Divine, it is precisely by failing that hermeneutics can best succeed. Having said this, I am not suggesting that the task of hermeneutics is dissolved thereby into what Pellauer typifies as "relativism." The degree to which relativism is an issue depends, first, on how the term itself is understood, and, second, on the nature of the text under discussion. In the former instance we must remember that in addition to its pejorative connotation it also enjoys a rather respectable and even critical place in the metaphysics of Whitehead and Hartshorne. In the latter instance, the book of Job is a text that defies most of the canons of ordinary criticism, as Pellauer points out, both in terms of what it meant and also in terms of what it means. Yet in spite of it all we encounter a text which, for all of its peculiarities, may still be viewed as being both autonomous and eminent in terms of its ability to address us powerfully.

Why is this the case? What is it about this text that enables it to reach beyond all the features of potential distanciation? The reason, it seems to me, is that this text addresses the concerns of all who attend to the problem of good and evil, justice, mercy, and the shape of things Eternal. But when the reader is faced with the task of appropriating the meaning of the text, when he "perceives himself," as Ricoeur puts it, "before the world of the text," then all the technical mechanisms and theories of interpretation fail or founder in the face of saying what it means. The reason for this, it seems to me, is that what it means cannot be said! This is not true, of course, in the case of most texts. But most texts do not have the quality of being eminent and few that can be so classified have the character of Job—certainly not in the religious literature of the West.

The failing or foundering of hermeneutics to which I allude is not, however, to be viewed as an end in itself, but rather as a critical stage in the process of the interpretation of religious texts, especially religious texts with the force and intensity of Job. It is a critical stage that I also see present in Ricoeur's position—at least up to a point. It will be recalled that Ricoeur speaks of the "obscurity" and the "ideality limits" as the dialectical foci of the hermeneutical circle, foci that have their analogues, in the problems of "sense" and "reference" respectively. These dialectical structures, as I have already pointed out, are especially interesting in the context of the book of Job because the resources of both movements are so completely exhausted. Hence we are left, it seems, with the need for a kind of wager, but here not merely the wager that can be identified with a movement from "descent" to "ascent" and the notion that the text must have a meaning. The wager to which I allude is entirely and completely religious and existential. In the final analysis, it is not really a wager at all since apart from the concrete experience of the conversion of the subject it cannot be objectified.

Perhaps this can be amplified a bit through reference to what Bernard Lonergan has elaborated in terms of the structures of self-transcendence, namely, "intellectual," "moral," and "religious conversion." The first two stages are dialectical, that is, they have to do with the movements from experience to understanding, and from understanding to judgment. The last stage, however, is not formally dialectical nor is it cumulative upon the realization of the other two. Religious conversion, or what Lonergan simply but profoundly describes as "being in love with God," is not the result of having mastered intellectual and moral conversion or, in our case, the "sense" and "reference" of a text. Job already understands these things and he still has a problem! If one wagers for love as one wagers the movement from understanding to judgment having exhausted all relevant questions as the preparation adequate for a kind of "leap," it is not "love" that one is leaping towards but something else. Religious conversion or "being in love with God," Fr. Lonergan tells us, more properly has to do with what is known as "falling in love" or, more precisely, with discovering, willy nilly, that one already is "in" love.

Now the language of "love" as we understand it is rather conspicuously absent from the book of Job. The structures, however, are quite present simply because, in the final analysis, all structures disappear! We are told in 42:5, for example, that now Job "sees" whereas he has only "heard" previously. "Hearing" in this instance clearly has to do with experiencing, knowing, judging, doing, and Job is the master of all these things. Why, then, does he not "see?" The "seeing" to which he alludes—and here hot on the heels of a very terrifying theophany—does not appear to have anything to do with the theophany itself or he would have said as much in 40:3—5. On the contrary, the Job we meet in 42:5 is the Job for whom all the resources of dialectical and objectifying thinking have *already* failed, and it is this failing or foundering that ultimately renders his harrowing experience salutary. Hence, Job's wager is not for more, for what he seeks is already there and has been all along. Thus the notion of wager also fails. I am reminded, finally, of some graffiti that I recently saw etched into the wall of the elevator in our office building. It asked, "How true, how true, is Nothing?" Since our building houses theology, classics, philosophy and religion, the graffiti tend to be rather ponderous and erudite! But the question was significant precisely in the sense that it could not be answered by objectifying discourse. What is the criteriology of "Nothing?" What is its sense and reference? Such a question is akin to asking what is the face of the *deus absconditus*?

Here again I think that Heidegger can be helpful to the degree that anyone can. Heidegger has told us repeatedly that "the step back is the step ahead," and by this he means that there must be a kind of renunciation of beings for Being to appear out of its concealment. By this he does not mean merely theoretical renunciation, but absolute renunciation as in Eckhart's sense of "the genuine poverty of the will," namely, "As long as one wills to do the will of God, and yearns for eternity and God, one is not really poor; for he who is poor wills nothing, knows nothing, wants nothing" (228). Clearly Being has *withdrawn* from Job, and Being does not appear out of its concealment until he has renounced all the devices of objectifying thinking and understanding. So it is that the Silence of Job *is* his testimony to Being.

WORK CONSULTED

Eckhart, Meister
    1941   *Meister Eckhart: A Modern Translation*. Trans. Raymond Blakney. New York: Harper and Row.

DECONSTRUCTION, PLURIVOCITY, AND SILENCE

Allan Patriquin
Beloit College

The debate between semiotics and the hermeneutical theory of Paul Ricoeur continues to be a productive arena into which to enter. Richard Jacobson, referring to himself as a post-structuralist semiotician, has shown how provocatively useful a new semiotic approach can be in his paper, "Satanic Semiotics, Jobian Jurisprudence." My own response to this paper draws upon Ricoeur's interpretation theory, and seeks to extend it by focusing on the interplay between language and silence in the book of Job. The aim here is to keep the debate alive by sustaining the conflict, but also the contact, between these two major hermeneutical enterprises.

Jacobson centers his discussion on a proposed link between poetics and politics. He asserts that control over language is the essence of power. He concludes that the authors of the book of Job wielded this power by depriving all of the book's characters of their actual voices by writing their speeches for them into the text. It is especially crucial to Jacobson's analysis that God was silenced through this process of deconstruction because Jacobson believes that divinity must be separated from justice: "Justice must stand apart from divinity to allow of a just world. Merge justice and divinity, and Yahweh is no better than Thrasymachus."

In order to actualize justice apart from divinity, Jacobson asserts the hermeneutic privilege, the right to interpret. For him, this privilege can only be exercised by deconstructing all of one's predecessors. This functions within the book of Job as a series of actions: Job deconstructs his friends' Deuteronomic theory of retribution, God deconstructs Job's elaborate legal defense, and the authors deconstruct God by replacing his living voice with a literary voice of their own composition. Whatever truth may be expressed within the book is, thus, rendered deliberately subjective, grounded in the exercise of autonomous freedom by each successive authority figure. The final attainment of justice without divinity occurs outside of the book in the interpreter's act of deconstructing the authors by saying what they meant. Iconoclasm becomes the prime hermeneutical method as persons seek to create their own independence. When God can no longer speak, then human beings can announce their freedom.

This is a powerful analysis. Its Nietzschean overtones confer a liberated, god-like status on each individual who is inevitably called to create his own world. Semiotic authority is marshalled against traditional authority, giving the enterprise a profoundly Oedipal character. Jacobson has touched upon fundamental themes which Ricoeur has also frequently addressed.

Over against this understanding of the need for and the process of deconstruction, the concept of plurivocity may be usefully juxtaposed. For Jacobson, the text of Job is, by definition, evidence of the absence of both Job and God. By contrast, Ricoeur's understanding of plurivocity argues that even written language retains the presence of many voices. In the case of the book of Job, Ricoeur's view acknowledges the authors' clear hand in composing all of the speeches. Nowhere in the text is there the prophetic formula, "Thus says the Lord," which would signal the authors' belief that they were recording actual divine words. But the levels of discourse within the text are not arranged in an ascending hierarchy of authority beginning with the conventional wisdom of Job's friends and ending with the pronouncements of the authors. Rather, the levels of discourse are dynamically interrelated; so much so, in fact, that the obscene inequities and insensibilities of the prose epilogue (which Jacobson rightly denounced as morally incommensurate with the loss of Job's first children) are shouted down by the lingering voice of God still questioning from the whirlwind and refusing to be silenced by the author's final injustice. The questioning God is unsuccessfully domesticated by the epilogue and its shallow doctrine of materialistic compensation. The God who interrogated Job lends his voice to all who would call the epilogue into question on moral grounds. Deconstruction does occur, but through the plurivocity of God, and probably of Job as well, against the writer of the epilogue.

While the semiotic approach is intentionally reductive in its search for the one authoritative voice which is, thereby, the one free voice, Ricoeur's emphasis on plurivocity affirms the freedom of language itself to say more than any author, or interpreter, can predetermine. Metaphorically speaking, the author of the epilogue is hoisted on the petard of the author of the speeches of Job and God in the earlier discourses. The poetics of authority occur within the language of the text, not exclusively outside of it in the control of either the authors or the book's interpreters. The plurivocity of language, if it is recognized as a fundamental element in the hermeneutical process, keeps all of a text's voices alive and speaking. An interpreter engages in the dialogue of the text, not in an authoritative monologue about what the text means at any one time. The world in front of the text emerges through this dynamic intercommunication with the world of the text and the world behind the text.

But there is also the silence. In the book of Job, Job places his hand over his mouth after hearing the first of God's magisterial questions. God himself is silent about his wager with the Satan and about the merits of Job's plea for justice. The text before us, for all of its tensive aliveness, is silently fixed in print for our eyes to read; only through language's call to our imaginations can the voices of the text be said to address us. And there is also the silence of every interpreter of this book, no one of whom seems able to explain its full meaning.

Jacobson understands the book as a call to freedom through linguistic acts of deconstruction. I agree that freedom is its final aim, but it is a freedom that is expressed not by the exercise of control over language, but rather a freedom symbolized in the surplus of meaning which exists because language is, utimately, free from the texts into which it is written. This freedom of language finds expression in its ability to interpret us. The fact that the book of Job has claimed our attention and prompted us to respond to it signifies its power to call us into dialogue with itself and others. It interprets us as actors in its drama. We may realize our freedom through a silent listening to the text's many voices, and through imaginative discourse with those still living voices. An interpreter must enter the silences of the book of Job as well as its speeches in order to experience the freedom of which it speaks.

Poetics finally frees us from the need to control language. The power of the book of Job lies in Job's experience of the presence of God in the whirlwind speeches, a presence which transcends his capacity for comprehension. Job does not attain autonomous freedom, but rather the knowledge of God articulated in his words of confession and obedience. The authority of the book of Job is its testimony that the experiences of justice and injustice cannot be transcended through language, or through any other means, but they can be endured within the dialectic of presence and absence in a freedom for language's fullness under the sign of the liberating silence.

www.ingramcontent.com/pod-product-compliance
Lightning Source LLC
Chambersburg PA
CBHW032301150426
43195CB00008BA/540